Little Parables of Life

JUDY L. GRENLEY, PhD

xulon
PRESS

This book is dedicated
in loving memory to my mother,
Jean Scott Lee

Contents

1. Jesus Arrived . . . and Right on Time
2. Timing Is Everything
3. Where's Dad?
4. Daddy Can Do It!
5. Walk like a Man
6. Growing Pains
7. Listen to the Head Coach
8. Life Is a Hike
9. Because He Can't Help Himself
10. God's Little Security Blanket
11. Cleanup on Aisle Three
12. The Boy Who Danced
13. A Father's Good Gift
14. Just Say No to Fear
15. Messengers of Comfort
16. Our Crowning Achievements
17. Do the Hokey Pokey
18. To the Rescue
19. Moving On Up
20. Famous Last Words

Acknowledgments

With much love and gratitude to:

Father, Son, and Holy Spirit—There is no life and certainly no
writing without You.
My husband, Michael, who always agrees to my projects and
endeavors—You are forever my sweet man.
Our children, Sally and Will—I hope you know how much you
are loved and what a blessing you both are.
Our son-in-law, Daniel—You are a treasure,
and I love how you love our daughter.
My extended family—Thank you to my favorite aunties, Janet
and Polly, and to all the Scott and Lee cousins.
My girlfriends and partners in crime: Cindy, Lorraine,
and Stephanie— Life is always better with "ya-yas."
Lee Ann Stauffer—Who encouraged me to write the original
newsletter.
Karen Davis—Who generously provided me
with my first audience.
Susan Wiser—Who brought out the Spirit in me.
The late Dr. Margaret Bomar—God's faithful servant and my
mentor who brought the Bible to life for me.
Norma Hill—My dear and true accountability partner.
Dr. Ron Hamm, Dr. Howie Cantrell, Carolyn Duffy, and all of my
friends and teachers at Life Development Institute—
I am grateful for your love and support.
The wonderful folks at Cedar Creek Yacht Club—

Thank you for your kindness and encouragement.
And last but not least, Jan Strawn—From God's lips to your ears,
thank you for being obedient.

This book belongs to all of you.
Thank you from the entirety of my heart.

Introduction

*T*his collection of writings began about twenty-five years ago as a column called *Judy's Joy* in the *Joyful Noises* monthly newsletter for the Tulip Grove Baptist Church Mother's Day Out program in Old Hickory, Tennessee. With the encouragement of the program's director, Karen Davis, and the generosity and interest of the staff and parents, I shared a monthly ditty about events in my life and how God had turned them into spiritual lessons. They developed into what I like to call my "kingdom metaphors," and the interest they sparked spurred me to keep writing what I experienced and what I learned from those experiences, and to turn them into a devotional.

These writings are largely evangelical and discipleship motivated. I feel they were inspired to uplift women, young mothers in particular, during a season of their lives when time is at a premium and quiet time is virtually nonexistent. I also feel that my writing has evolved over the years and might now appeal to Christian women and men of all ages and stages of life. It is about the "God life"; I hope you will be able to relate and that it brings you a bit of joy, peace, and maybe a few tears and giggles along the way. If anything, this book will serve as proof that God truly is in the details. Thank you for reading *Little Parables of Life*.

And a Little Child Shall Lead Them

Isaiah 11:6

Jesus Arrived . . . and Right on Time

And Mary said, "My soul magnifies the Lord, and my spirit has rejoiced in God my Savior. For He has regarded the lowly state of His maidservant; for behold, henceforth all generations will call me blessed."
Luke 1:46–48

When our daughter, Sally, was born six and a half weeks premature, the doctors from the neonatal intensive care unit (NICU) whisked her away before I could hold or touch her. Because she weighed in at only three pounds and fifteen ounces, her birth was an emergency. The doctors had to examine her closely to make sure that her lungs and all bodily functions were in good working order. Consequently, I didn't mind too much that I didn't get to see her very well, except for a quick glance at a tiny scrunched-up face peeking out from under a little striped knit cap, before she left the delivery room.

While I was in the recovery room, several reports came back to me from the NICU that my daughter was indeed breathing on her own and causing quite a commotion with very loud, high-pitched howls. They were not doubtful at all that her lungs were perfectly healthy. Nonetheless, I wasn't going to be completely satisfied until I held her in my arms and examined that tiny little body for myself.

After recovery, the nurses wheeled me down to the NICU on a gurney and, in spite of the tight squeeze, parked me right next to Sally's incubator. There she was. She could be held easily in one hand. Her thighs were smaller around than the narrow end of a medium-sized carrot, and the skin on her tiny fingers was so thin that you could see the shadow of the bones within them.

The nurses opened the incubator from the side, and I slid my baby onto the gurney, right beside me. Then I did something that all mothers have done from the beginning of time: I stripped my baby of every stitch of clothing and took inventory of every part. It was one of those moments in time that seems as though it is in slow motion. That single moment felt like an eternity, as though the minutes and seconds were hovering over my head, waiting for my permission to commence ticking again. I'll never forget that moment as long as I live—the first moment I truly felt like a mother.

I have no doubt that in those first moments after Jesus' birth, Mary felt the very same way and did all the things new mothers do: counted fingers and toes, kissed those sweet little crying lips, and shaded His eyes from the brightness of His new surroundings. She felt all those same feelings—those gut-deep emotions that come with knowing that you now have the greatest responsibility in life. She was, after all, a mother.

Mary, though, had a much greater responsibility than we do as new parents, for in her arms she was holding her very own Savior. She would have to raise and prepare Him for a future that we would never, could never, fathom for our little ones—a destiny of suffering and dying for all mankind.

Sally came early, before we were fully prepared to receive her into our lives, but Jesus came right on time. We don't have to be prepared to receive Him into our lives; He wants us to come to Him just as we are. And when we do, that peace that we all long for comes to us as well. Do you know Him? Do you know who He is? It's not too early, and it's not too late. Now is the perfect time to find out.

Prayer: *What a wonderful privilege it is to be a mother. Thank You, Father, for the gift of eternal life that You have made available to us through faith in Your Son, Jesus Christ. Your timing is absolutely perfect. Amen.*

Timing Is Everything

A man's heart plans his way, but the LORD directs his steps.
Proverbs 16:9

"My water has broken," I said to Mike when I called him at work. "I'll be right there" was his answer. In the next thirty minutes, I packed up Sally and sent her home with a friend, called my mom, and packed my bag. For the second time in my life, I was giving birth six and a half weeks prematurely. We had been down this road before.

Mike pulled quickly into the driveway, and in five minutes, we were on the interstate, hurtling at warp speed toward the hospital. Now here is where I teach you a little bit about my husband. I want you to understand that I'm not complaining; I love him just the way God sent him to me. He is, however, one of *those* people: the A-type, OCD, "everything has to be in my day planner" type of person. If it is not written on the to-do list, then it is not happening. If it is on the list, Mike's head is not hitting the pillow until everything is checked off. Now, I like a neat and ordered life myself, but I am Miss Loosey-Goosey compared to him. Early on, I learned to preserve my energy and take it steady, and I could still get the job done. I'm the tortoise, and Mike is the hare—on steroids. He always has been, and still is.

When Sally was born, she came at about six in the evening. Now that we were on the way to the hospital to have our second child, Mike was chuckling to himself because it was midmorning and he was sure that we were *not* going to be one of those couples who had to stay up all night to have one of those "wee hours of the morning" babies. I dryly reminded him that this was, as always, out of our control. Plus, I hadn't even had my first labor pain yet.

Two days later, we were still at the hospital and waiting for that first pain. My husband's world had been sufficiently rocked. He might as well have torn those two pages out of his day planner, because nothing was going as planned. The second night, Mike announced to everyone that he and Sally were going home to feed the dogs and get a good night's rest in their own beds, but then the first pain finally hit me about nine o'clock. Ignoring that fact, he proceeded to attempt a follow-through with his plan.

To put it mildly, my mother saw it differently; she made it very clear to him, in no uncertain terms, that there might be a lot of things happening that night, but going home was not one of them. Will was on the way, and no one was going anywhere. It was time to erase that agenda from the day planner and make a new plan. My husband, realizing he had no choice in the matter, changed his plan of action. Will was born at 2:55 a.m. in the dead stillness of the predawn hours . . . and who says God doesn't have a sense of humor?

It's a good thing to plan and have order in your life, but if God is not doing any of the ordering, then you will find yourself on that treadmill of life, moving constantly but getting nowhere. I can assure you—it will be frustrating. The primary and most important plan is His plan. He has a purpose for us, and when we get on board with what He foresees written in the Book of Life, then we can relax, slow down, and stick with His program. It *will* get done, all in His timing.

Prayer: *Father, I think it is awesome that from the foundation of the world, You knew me and had a plan and a purpose for me. I am excited to see all the good things You will bring to my life in Your timing. Amen.*

Where's Dad?

And the ransomed of the LORD shall return, and come to Zion with singing, with everlasting joy on their heads. They shall obtain joy and gladness, and sorrow and sighing shall flee away.
Isaiah 35:10

There were a lot of days when our son, Will, got off the school bus in the afternoon and both my husband and I would be home to greet him after his long day at school. We would have a lot of fun teasing him by standing at the door together, arm in arm, waving at him in a very goofy fashion as he made his way down the driveway from the school bus. I know he was probably praying that none of his friends would see his demented parents welcoming him home in this way. But at the same time, he would have this huge and embarrassed grin on his face, and we could tell that he felt special, knowing that we were truly glad to have him back home with us again. Even though deep down Will liked the warm receptions, he would often complain about us being so enthusiastically over the top about his coming home. I guess I wasn't very reassuring in reminding him that he needed to be thankful for the parents that God had given him, and that he just better get used to it because we were always going to be happy to see him come home.

Some days it would work out that only my husband, Mike, would be the one to greet Will. When this was the case, Mike would walk all the way out to the end of the driveway, taking Will's backpack from him to give his shoulders some relief from all his books, and ask him about his day. They would have quite the animated conversation as Will related the events of his day to his dad. On the rare occasion when Mike was not home when Will arrived, the first words out of his mouth were "Where's Dad?" Coming home was just not the same when Dad wasn't there.

There's a story in the Bible of a prodigal son, a wayward child who took off and left his family, taking his inheritance with him and then squandering it all away. Finding himself in dire straits—dirty, homeless, and no longer able to care for himself—he made his way back home, tail tucked between his legs. Instead of returning to find a judgmental and aloof reception, however, he experienced his father literally running out to greet him. His father hugged him and rewarded him with a new robe, new sandals, a costly ring, and a great banquet (Luke 15:11–32).

I often think about that story and how remarkable it is that home and family is (or should be) synonymous with forgiveness, unconditional love, and a welcome mat that is always out. What if the prodigal son had come home to an empty house? What if there had been no loving father to greet him? What would have become of him?

Regardless of what kind of reception our earthly families give us, we have a heavenly Father who always welcomes us with open arms. He is quick to forgive and forget, and He delights in our return to Him. While we are still residents of planet earth, we can return to Him only in our hearts, but someday we will shed our earthly bodies and return to Him by way of our spirits. When that time comes, I believe He will rush to greet us with a warm smile, a huge hug, and a great feast, just like the father in the prodigal son story. We will be home, and we won't have to ask, "Where's Dad?" What a great day that will be!

Prayer: *Lord, how amazing is the unconditional love You have for Your children! I am blessed, Father, to know that You will always welcome me home. Amen.*

Daddy Can Do It!

But without faith it is impossible to please Him for he who comes to
God must believe that He is and that He is a rewarder
of those who diligently seek Him.
Hebrews 11:6

When I was a little girl, I thought my daddy could do or fix anything. If I wanted something, I asked him. If I wanted him to build something, I'd tell him. If I broke it, I'd immediately take it to him. My confidence in Daddy was enormous, and no matter how big the challenge, I knew he'd come through for me.

There used to be a commercial for a nationwide chain of home-improvement stores that reminded me of that fact every time I saw it. It featured a little boy talking with his friends, bragging that his daddy was going to build him a tree house. He told his friends, "My dad is a genius; he can build anything!" He went on to say that the tree house would be the best ever, that it would have a balcony, windows . . . everything. The little boy's confidence in his dad did not waver.

Then, in the next scene, we'd see the dad at the home-improvement store. Contrary to the faith of the little boy, the dad had absolutely no confidence in himself; he obviously had never undertaken a building challenge of this magnitude before, and he was asking the advice of an employee of the store. He was very unsure of himself, but the employee reassured him that the instructions were simple and he could do it. Finally, the commercial concluded with the little boy and his dad camping out in the finished tree house, complete with windows and a balcony, and the little boy saying very earnestly, "Thanks, Dad!" The dad responded simply with a warm smile of love and satisfaction.

As an adult, I now realize that my daddy couldn't do everything; he was human. I'm sure that he had a lot of the same reservations as the dad depicted in the commercial when it came to coming through for his child. But I do have another Father, a heavenly one, who is completely confident that He can do for me what no one else can do. He is more than a genius—He created genius—and He always comes through for me. If I want or need something, I ask Him. If I want Him to build something into my life, I step aside and cooperate with Him as He does much of the work. If I mess something up, I tell Him I'm sorry and ask Him to give me the wisdom to work out the problems I've created for myself and to give me strength to deal with the consequences. I have the confidence that there is no task too big or project too complex for my heavenly Father. He never fails to come through for me.

This confidence in God is a thing called "faith." It goes beyond just believing that God can; it takes us to the place where we know for certain that without fail, He keeps His Word and His promises to us, always. We trust in His character and ability more than in what we see, hear or feel. It is pleasing to Him when we have that kind of faith and it produces results in our lives.

I make it a point every day to earnestly say, "Thank You, Father." And then I imagine that He is smiling lovingly back at me, pleased with the trust I have placed in Him. We really do have a Daddy who can do anything!

Prayer: *I am so blessed to be able to call You "Father," and I am so grateful to be included in Your family. I am in awe of Your faithfulness, and it is my prayer that my trust and confidence in You will continue to grow with each new day. Amen.*

Walk like a Man

He who has seen Me has seen the Father.
John 14:9

I have always found preschoolers fascinating. I taught them for many years in a Mother's Day Out program. Aside from mothering, it was the most rewarding and exhausting of all the work I've ever done. Yes, preschoolers are incredibly interesting human beings, and they have much to teach us if we will just take the time to watch and learn.

Years ago I observed a neighbor's child, a young boy of about three years of age, playing by himself in his front yard. He was off saving another planet or rescuing a princess in distress, riding off into the sunset on his Big Wheel. He was totally unaware of his surroundings or my observation of him, and he was completely immersed in the freedom of being himself (or someone else), innocent and unencumbered by the cares of life. It was sweet and wholesome, and I found myself rather jealous of him in the midst of his oblivious reverie.

A while later, I noticed the little guy coming out of the house with his dad. He seemed thrilled to be going on this special errand, just two guys on the road together. I watched as he followed his dad out to the car, realizing something was very different about him from before. His walk had changed. The carefree toddling skip was gone, and now his stride matched that of his grown-up father's—a near-perfect imitation of his dad's masculine gait. The two moved together down the sidewalk towards the car, seamlessly in sync, the father and his miniature shadow. It dawned on me how incredibly touching this was. The little boy admired his father so much that he had developed a flawless imitation of him. Earlier he had been pretending to be a hero, and now he was imitating the real hero in his life. My heart melted as I watched him follow his daddy to the car and climb into his car seat, and off they went.

God has given us a very clear picture of what He is like, and that picture is Jesus. We can tell what God is all about just by studying Jesus. He walked and talked and acted like His Daddy. He showed us who God is and how God loves us, through His own words and actions.

For many of us, one of the big mysteries of life has always been, who is God and what is He like? There is no mystery here. God has revealed

Himself through His Son, and all we have to do is take a look into the Word of God to discover all we need to know about our Creator. It is there that we see the boy and the man, Jesus, walking like His Daddy and showing us how to walk like Him while we tread this earth as well.

Prayer: *My heart's desire, Lord, is to know You and, as a result of that intimate understanding, become more like You every day. Amen.*

Growing Pains

But grow in the grace and knowledge of our Lord and Savior, Jesus Christ. To Him be the glory both now and forever. Amen.
2 Peter 3:18

Did you ever have growing pains in your legs when you were a child? I had them, and I remember how painful they were. Over the years, I've realized that there is more than one kind of growing pain. It seems that whenever there is growth of any kind, there is discomfort. I think that must be one of the reasons we are so resistant to change—it's uncomfortable!

I remember when my children were small and going through all their preschool phases. Just when I thought I had one phase licked, another one would come along and I was in the dark again. I eventually figured out that I had to learn to adjust and go with the flow. As a result, my children's growth spurts became my growth spurts too.

I now realize that I probably made those phases harder on the children than they needed to be. I didn't have "by the book" kids (who does?). With little or no forewarning, they would realize they were big enough to do something new, but they weren't quite sure how to do it. Some adamant exploration was required, and they needed guidance. I, however, was usually stuck in the routines of the prior phase. Sometimes I was afraid they might get hurt in this new phase, and other times I was just slow in figuring out what they needed to navigate through it. It had to be frustrating for them; it certainly was for me. No wonder the word *no* or the phrase *Me do it!* was heard so often. Yes, growth is uncomfortable.

I hate to be the bearer of tough news, but this cycle of surprise, adjustment, change, and growth does not end, even when our children become adults. They (and we) don't stop growing and changing, and they never fail to surprise us. Our real job is to accept them and how special and wonderful they are at every phase and to pray that we all come out of it somehow unscathed. It keeps us humble . . . and on our toes!

I often refer to God as the perfect parent, and because He is, He's extremely capable of relating to us. Because He became a man—Jesus—He also experienced the difficulties of growth spurts. He really understands us— *gets* us. He lived the human experience, and He is never surprised by us. If we allow it, He will use the cycles of change and the circumstances of life to grow us up, and the result is that we will become more like Him. Change and growth are rarely fun, just as the growing pains of our youth were not fun. But just as in our physical and emotional growth, they are very necessary for our spiritual development as well. Isn't it wonderful that we have that perfect parent who understands and accepts us and is well able to love us through it?

Prayer: *Give me the grace, Father, to bear the discomfort of the growth You have laid before me, and may the results be pleasing to You. Amen.*

Listen to the Head Coach

Now therefore, if you will indeed obey My voice and keep My covenant,
then you shall be a special treasure to Me above all people;
for all the earth is Mine.
Exodus 19:5

When he was growing up, our son, Will, loved playing Little League baseball. In actuality, it was mostly about wearing the uniform, but the game was fun and a good life experience too. It was one of the highlights of his year when the season started—the uniform was new, after all. There were a lot of life lessons that came out of our baseball years with Will, but the one thing I like to focus on when it comes to this time in our lives is that it taught me the importance of listening and being obedient to God.

There is a sort of hierarchy in Little League baseball—at least there is in our neck of the woods—and it goes like this: There is the head coach, several assistant coaches, the team mom, and of course the team. Then on the sidelines, there are the parents. In the stands, my enjoyment of the game (and watching Will straighten his uniform out in right field) was often distracted by the behavior of the other parents, and more often than not, it wasn't pretty.

For some of these folks, their approach to the team-sports concept was dramatic, over the top, and, at least from my perspective, a little bizarre. Many of these spectator parents felt compelled to "coach" from the bleachers. More times than not, their agendas were completely in opposition to that of the head coach. He was much more experienced and had an understanding of the game that they didn't, yet they would still yell from the sidelines, directing their children (and many times, other people's children) to go here, go there, catch the ball, stop, run, slide, etc.

Because of the parental interference from the sidelines, the children became confused and couldn't hear what the coach, the true authority on the field, was directing them to do. The result was that the kids would mess up and get an out or make an error. It was important to the game that the parents lined up with what the coach was doing so that the children would learn to listen to him. Then the true expert on the field could teach them the nuances of the game and how to win or lose with spunk, spirit, and grace.

God has bestowed upon us an awesome privilege and responsibility in raising our children. On the field of life, we need to line ourselves up with the real authority and in the process teach our children to listen to and obey the head coach, Father God. Ultimately, on this field, it will give them an advantage and hopefully prevent many errors so that they won't find themselves out of the game.

Obedience is listening and following through, and the best way to teach our children this is by example. As my children grew, I tried to make it a priority to listen to my "head coach" so that I wouldn't give them mixed signals about what they were to do and not do in the big game of life. Eventually we all come to the time when we have to send our children out into the world to play the game for themselves, hoping that they have learned, in spite of our own shortcomings, to listen to the "head coach" and do what He says without question.

Prayer: *Father, teach me to recognize Your voice, to follow Your lead, and to walk in Your ways. Amen.*

Life Is a Hike

Therefore, humble yourselves under the mighty hand of God, that He
may exalt you in due time, casting all your care upon Him,
for He cares for you.
1 Peter 5:6–7

When the children were young and our time constraints were fewer, we would take several days each spring and fall to go on a day hike with them. We would pack a lunch, including the all-too-important toilet paper, and drive to a hiking trail in a state park and just walk and soak in the nature. The kids were, of course, much more energetic than dear old Mom and Dad, and they literally hopped, skipped, and jumped most of the way to our destination and back.

It was easier for us to pack our lunch and all the essentials in just one backpack, and my husband, Mike, was the designated carrier of our provisions. Of course, within his role as the dad, his duties also included carrying one or both of the children at different intervals on our walk. The mom character in this little scenario (me!) was doing well just to get herself down the trail and back free of blisters, sunburn, heatstroke, or a sprained ankle.

Often, usually every ten feet or so, our children would find little souvenirs along the path, such as a rock, a bird's feather, a flower, etc. Will especially loved the rocks, and he kept a box full of them under his bed to show off all his hard pioneering on the rugged trail. These souvenirs would be picked up here and there and placed in the family backpack, and Mike would continue to carry it throughout the hike.

When we arrived back at the car, we would empty out the backpack, inspect everything thoroughly, and usually leave behind almost everything, save a rock or two that was to be added to the under-the-bed collection. We were always exhausted after these hikes, and Mike was the one who ultimately had just enough energy left to drive us home, unload the car, and then make us all a pizza for dinner. He would see the day through to the very end, appearing tireless in his appointed task.

In many ways, life is just like those day hikes. The difficulty in the walk is dependent upon the austerity of the trail and who is carrying you and your backpack. My personal trail has had its share of bumps and perils, and at some point on my journey, I have chosen not to carry the load myself. Along the way, I have needed to hitch a ride a time or two when I became weary or the going got tough. Jesus has carried my "backpack" full of my necessities, and He has carried the "rocks" and "souvenirs" that I gathered along the way. He has carried me too—and still does.

Someday Jesus will take me all the way home. When I get to the end of the path, we'll clean out that backpack together. We'll throw away the souvenirs that aren't worth keeping, and what is left will be the most beautiful of my mementos—the treasures of my life that I will want to keep forever.

Jesus never tires of carrying your backpack. No matter how long the trail, no matter how many rocks you hand over to Him for safekeeping, He can take it. He'll carry it all the way home for you.

Are you holding on to some nonessentials that would best be left behind? He'll take them, if you are willing to hand them over. You can do it right now; you don't have to wait until the end of the hike to lighten the load. The Bible instructs us to cast all our cares upon Him because He cares for us. (1 Peter 5:7) It's the truth, it is His character, and wouldn't it be wonderful if we all had a lighter load to prove it?

Prayer: *What a relief it is to know that You carry us when we need You to, that You care for us and encourage us to leave all the nonessentials with You. Life can be hard, but You, Father, are always good. Amen.*

Because He Can't Help Himself

For God is love.
1 John 4:8

If you have ever been a parent or grandparent, then you know that overwhelming sense of profound and utter love you get when you watch that child sleep. I can remember the day we brought Sally home from the hospital. On the way home, we had to stop at the store to pick up diapers and other essential provisions for this new member of our little family. It was February and cold outside, so Mike left Sally and me in the warmth of the car while he ran in to get what we needed. She was in her car seat, and she was so tiny that she had to have several receiving blankets rolled up and tucked in around her to keep her secured. She was sleeping, and I could not take my eyes off her.

They say seeing is believing, but I could not wrap my mind around the fact that this child was finally here, that we were sharing a car ride and a mundane stop at the grocery store together—and that she was all mine. Here, the greatest gift I could ever imagine receiving, was in the flesh, right in front of me. The emotions I was experiencing were unlike anything I had ever felt before, and I knew that no matter how hard I tried, I would never be able to stop myself from feeling that way again.

I picked up those small fingers, and they lightly clamped around mine. She squeaked out a little sigh, her breaths, even and deep. This was wonder, this was peace, and this was love. If there ever had been, there was now absolutely no doubt of God or His incredible love for me.

The Bible says this about what real love is: "Love is patient, love is kind; love is not envious, or boastful, or arrogant, or rude. It does not insist on its own way; it is not irritable or resentful; it does not rejoice in wrongdoing but rejoices in the truth. It bears all things, believes all things, hopes all things, endures all things" (1 Corinthians 13:4–7). This is the very nature of the Creator. He loves us in this way, and we can only hope to aspire to this kind of love in our parenting and other relationships. God loves us because He *is* love, and when you *are* something, you just can't help doing what you are. In God's case, it's love. His love for us is not based on what we do or how we perform. It is based on who and what He is—love.

I have revisited those initial feelings of profound motherly love many times over the years in raising my children. I've watched them sleep too many times to count and at various stages of their lives. The feeling really doesn't go away. It becomes a part of you and who you are, and there is not one act, argument, or difficulty that can ever make it disappear. How much more long-lived, powerful, and intense must be the Father's love for us! It is beyond our imagination and comprehension. It just is because He is.

Prayer: *Father, the love I have for my children is so inadequate in comparison to the love You have for me. I am grateful that in my very often unlovable state, You can't help but love me anyway. I find great security in this truth about You. Amen.*

God's Little Security Blanket

To everything there is a season, a time for every purpose
under heaven: . . . a time to weep, and a time to laugh;
a time to mourn and a time to dance.
Ecclesiastes 3:1, 4

The thing about having friends, good friends, is that we must share not only their joys, but their sorrows as well. Years ago a dear friend of mine suffered the greatest loss of all when her twenty-seven-year-old son passed away suddenly. I found myself attending the funeral of a young person, and it was the worst. I hate funerals anyway, but after the death of my mother, which had occurred several years earlier, I found that they stirred up powerful emotions that I hoped I had finally put to rest. Funerals, especially those of sudden deaths, had become much tougher for me to attend.

As I sat in the chapel waiting for the service to begin, I prayed that I would be able to resist being too emotional. I wanted to be strong, and I didn't want to feel those old feelings of deep loss that recurred from time to time, especially at funerals. But God didn't answer my prayer in the way I hoped.

The young man who had passed away left behind a large, loving family: a devoted grandmother, two loving parents, a young, beautiful wife, and an adorable little angel of a daughter around the age of five. As the family entered the chapel after privately saying good-bye to their loved one, the old and very familiar look of shock, disbelief, grief, and sickening loss was very apparent on their faces. Those old feelings came flooding back, and my heart sank. But then God faithfully did what He always does. He showed me who He is and His wonderful provision in a very unexpected way.

I focused my attention on the little daughter as she was carried into the chapel by her mother, her arms clasped tightly about her mama's neck, taking in the magnitude of the event with big eyes, memorizing faces and emotions that she didn't understand. She had a sad look, sensing a great loss in her life but not really comprehending what it was all about. Once seated, she remained in her mama's lap, but facing backward toward the congregation. Then, as the music played and the people wept, something changed in her and in me.

I saw this little girl stroke her mother's neck as if to comfort her, to let her know, "I'm still here. I'll be with you always." A tiny, peaceful smile came across her face, and she got down, walked to the aisle, and began to dance. It wasn't misbehavior; it was a five-year-old, on the worst day of her young life, indicating to me and all who would notice that "all is well—I can still dance." It wasn't disrespectful or sacrilegious. It was innocence, it was trust and safety, and it was comfort.

I still continued to weep, but not from the old anguish that had come back to revisit me. My tears were a "thank you" to God for reminding me that in Him there is always comfort, always peace and security; that no matter what my circumstances or even if it is absolutely the worst day of my life, He is there and that there will always be a time to dance, just because of Him. When we have the faith of a child, all that He has for us becomes real, and truly the comfort we need comes to us, not by seeking it out, but by giving it. When we do, then it will once again be time to dance.

Prayer: *Father, thank You for Your comforting and abiding presence. Please help me to always be mindful of those around me who need to be comforted, and use me to send Your comfort to them. Amen.*

Cleanup on Aisle Three

For My yoke is easy and My burden is light.
Matthew 11:30

One day I stopped at the grocery store to pick up a few things for dinner, and as usual, I was in a hurry. As I rounded the corner from one aisle to the next, I found myself in the school supply section, and in front of me was . . . an opportunity.

A little girl about the age of six had been handling some of the small spiral notebooks and had accidentally knocked loose the wire rack that held the merchandise in place on the shelves. She was holding the rack and unsuccessfully trying to keep the merchandise from slipping onto the floor. She was crying to herself, little tears streaming down her face. The child was obviously panicked and didn't have a clue about what to do.

I admit that I was feeling a little irritated because I was running late, but I put my shopping basket and purse down on the floor and offered to help her anyway. I told her not to worry, that we could fix it together, but in her panic and frustration, she cried out and informed me that there was nothing we could do, that it was all going to fall to the floor. The situation was so big and hopeless in her mind that all she could do was assume a disastrous conclusion.

I held the rack for her as she pulled all the notebooks together into piles and stacked them up; then her sister came around the corner and began to help her as well. I kept offering words of encouragement and comfort, and it was not long until the little girl was no longer fretting and crying. We became a team and got the mess cleaned up, and I told her I would tell someone at the front desk so that the shelf could be repaired. The look of relief on her little face was incredible—a total transformation from the little girl I had discovered just a few minutes earlier.

We all sometimes get ourselves into predicaments that seem too big, too overwhelming for us to handle. Often we just panic and cry out, not knowing where to turn. But Jesus will bring calm and order to any situation, if we let Him. There is no problem or challenge that is too big for Him to handle. When we decide to let Him take over, things no longer seem hopeless and desperate. We stop looking at how big the problem is, and we begin to see how small it looks in contrast to the One who is handling it. He bears our burdens with us because He loves us.

If we can just remember to turn it over to Him, He will go right to work and lighten the load; peace will then come to us, and anxiety will flee. Are you bearing a burden that you aren't equipped to handle alone? I challenge you to give it to Jesus today, and then just wait and see what happens next!

Prayer: *Father, please prompt my spirit to turn to You immediately when there is a burden too great for me to bear alone. Help me to remember that You are as close as the whisper of Your name and that You care about all the things that concern me. Amen.*

The Boy Who Danced

Let them praise His name with the dance; let them sing praises to Him with the timbrel and harp. Psalm 149:3

I am absolutely convinced that one of the best things we ever did for our children was to introduce them to dance. Sally began dance classes at age three when the doctor insisted we involve her in an activity or sport that would help build muscle and increase her appetite. Will was about five when he started dance, not because he wanted to follow in his sister's footsteps, but because "the girls will like me." Both of our kids had natural talent (my dad was a talented dancer, but I guess it skipped a generation!). Add in many years of excellent instruction and practice, and what we got was a daughter who is a gifted choreographer and dance studio owner and a son who is a multitalented performer.

Will, in all his wisdom, will be the first to tell you that his sister is the dancer and he is just a performer who dances. And it's true. Sally is graceful and fluid, and her timing and technique are impeccable. Will lives to be on stage and has never had a single qualm about the fact that he is a male who dances. What we've always loved about our children's dancing is that they love to dance together; they do it well, and they aren't competitive with each other about it. It bonded them in a way that most brothers and sisters don't get to bond. When they dance together, it truly is art and of course gives us something to brag about.

The thing about a boy who dances and dances well is that he draws a lot of attention, even without meaning to. I have wondered why this is so and thought that maybe it is just because it is so uncommon. After further contemplation, however, I now believe that it probably goes deeper than that. I've come to the conclusion that it is almost a spiritual thing of sorts. You feel it more than you view it. When Will dances, there is an abandon that you sense. He seems to lose his self-awareness and connects with a force within himself, a deeply masculine and earthy grace. It is humble, proficient, an unnameable quality that comes from deep within to the outside. It is refreshing and stimulating to the beholder—at least it is to this beholder.

There was another man who, when he danced, must have displayed this quality. His act of abandon was one of worship, and there was a complete disregard for himself or his reputation. This man's name was David. In 2 Samuel 6, you will find the account of how he celebrated when the Ark of the Covenant was brought to Jerusalem. By this time in his life, David was a grown man, the anointed and crowned king of Israel, and had a vast reputation as a great and fierce warrior as well as a fair, benevolent, and dignified ruler. Yet he set himself aside, abandoned his kingly dignity, and, in complete and utter worship, displayed his immense joy as he danced before his God through the streets of Jerusalem in what today would be considered his underwear!

How often do we abandon ourselves, set ourselves completely aside so that our passion for God is displayed in such an intense and pure way? True worship is lifestyle, not just how we act in church. It's about our attitude and devotion to God. How deep is your sellout? Do you desire Him in His fullness every day, not just on Sundays? The focus has to be on God, not on what others are doing. It can't be self-conscious; the self must be lost. When David was in that state of sheer abandonment, he was not the one producing the joy that he was displaying—God was. David was just reacting purely to it. It was humble and came from someplace deep within him.

God wants all of us. He gave us all of Himself. To give Him any less will not yield what He wants to produce in us, and we cannot experience Him in the fullness of joy that is available to us until we truly do surrender all. That charismatic quality that we see in a boy who dances can be seen in our lives on an even grander scale every day as the result of our full and complete relinquishment to God. It shines through, and it is joy-producing and cannot be mistaken for anything else. John the Baptist said, "He [Jesus] must increase, but I must decrease" (John 3:30). Are you willing to risk it all and decrease yourself to experience Him more fully today? The dance will begin the minute you do.

Prayer: *Lord, in my daily life, my body doesn't always feel like dancing, but my heart is certainly willing. Help me to be mindful of the great joy I can always find in Your presence. Amen.*

A Father's Good Gift

*If you then, being evil, know how to give good gifts to your children,
how much more will Your Father who is in heaven give good
things to those who ask Him!*
Matthew 7:11

Mike and I had the wonderful privilege of teaching a tenth-grade Sunday school class for several years. Many wonderful and memorable children came through the class during that time, and as it is for many teachers, we learned as much, if not more, from our students as they learned from us. This is the story of one such lesson.

On the occasion of his graduation, one of our former Sunday school students received a very special gift from his dad: a guitar that he had custom made himself for his oldest son. Now this particular guitar wasn't just some crude, homemade, thrown-together instrument. It was very carefully made from the finest wood, meticulously cut as close to perfection as human hands could produce, sanded to utter smoothness, polished to gleaming brightness, inlaid with fine mother-of-pearl and abalone, and tuned to a beautiful resonant perfection.

A burning bush that had been designed by this boy's brother was carved into the wood, and inlaid mother-of-pearl flames and flying embers shone and flickered up the neck of the guitar. On the inside, carefully and deliberately placed there before the guitar was glued together, were the signatures of the father who built it and the son who received it. The names could not be seen from the outside, but for all eternity they were sealed there as a memorial of a priceless, selfless gift from father to son to earmark a rite of passage and a season of life that was fading away.

This young man was very musically gifted. I had heard him play on many occasions, and I had always been impressed by his skill. But the first time I heard him strike a note on that beautiful work of art, I could hear the sound of love floating from those strings and hanging in the air like a golden cloud. He had never played as well as he did on that amazing gift from his father. I am sure he had never doubted the love of his father, but for the rest of his life, he now had a precious physical evidence of it. What a special treasure!

God gifts us with so much throughout our lifetimes, but what He gave us in Jesus is indeed priceless. Before the foundation of the world, the Father carefully constructed a plan to save mankind by sending His precious and perfect Son. That plan was sealed, delivered, and became a physical presence here on earth, a one-of-a-kind gift to us that said, "I love you." After His long, meticulous work was completed, Jesus returned to the Father, but the signature He left behind can be found in our hearts and is evidenced by the imprint we leave and the beautiful and joyful sound that we make while we are here. Be glad you have a Father who loves you so much and lavishes you with many, many precious gifts.

Prayer: *How amazed I am, Lord, at Your limitless kindness and generosity and how extravagantly you pour out Your love to Your children. May I always be a gracious and thankful steward of all that You bestow upon me. Amen.*

Just Say No to Fear

*For God has not given us a spirit of fear, but of power
and of love and of a sound mind.*
2 Timothy 1:7

I always said that when my husband and I became parents, we realized what real fear was. The moment our daughter was born, we recognized that we now possessed something that had taken our hearts captive, and with that came a dread and a fear of anything ever happening to her. Much later we learned that this original fear was just for the minor leagues. The *real* fear came along when our teenager began driving solo.

A few days after earning her driver's license, Sally took off all by herself for the first time in a little car we had refurbished for her. As I stood at the kitchen window, with my hand over my mouth, heart in my throat, and fighting back a deluge of tears, my mind raced back to all those "firsts" over the years that I had dreaded, prepared for, and then survived.

There were those first steps and all the bumps and bruises it took to learn to walk, the first tooth that was pulled, the first solo bike ride, the first overnight sleepover away from home. Then there was the first day of "big school." She had looked so tiny in that big classroom. I remembered watching her get on the school bus by herself for the first time and crossing the street all by herself. I remembered the first time she went on an out-of-town school trip without one of us along as a chaperone—that was a biggie for me. There was the first day of junior high, when her "old" parents weren't allowed to walk her to her class anymore. Then there was the first time I let her boyfriend drive her to church, just the two of them. And prom—I cried for two days over that one.

Parenting is not for "fraidy-cats," that's for sure. Fear is the opposite of faith, and we have to parent our children in faith in order to get through all of those "firsts" intact. We have to have faith in ourselves and what we have taught our children, but ultimately, we have to have faith in God. We have to learn to trust Him; after all, He sees our children when we don't. The real test of our faith comes by letting our children move on when we can't see the outcome, but God can. I don't believe that we can have peace in our parenting in any other way.

I'll be honest—over the years, there have been many times that I didn't want to trust God with my children. That "mama bear" in me wanted to say, "I can protect them better than God can." However, the spiritual reality is, that is just not true. Nobody can protect them, care for them, or love them better than He can. After all, He created them.

The parenting role has been a very effective instrument in my spiritual development. If I can trust God with my children, I can trust Him with anything. I'm hoping that if you are still in that season of raising children or about to embark upon it, you will trust God with all the "firsts" that are ahead of you. You and your children will grow together in ways that you can't imagine.

Prayer: *Forgive me, Lord, for all those times I didn't trust You with my children. Even in my fear, You blessed me so completely. Now that my children are grown and no longer under my watchful care, I know they are under Yours, and that gives me great peace. Amen.*

Messengers of Comfort

I will not leave you orphans; I will come to you.
John 14:18

During my many years of teaching preschool, it was a common occurrence for me to learn something new about God, myself, or others through the words or actions of a preschooler. One day, when substituting for another teacher, another wonderful lesson from Father came my way.

At group time that morning, a little girl was moving her chair into the circle, tripped, fell, and bumped her head. It was a nasty little bump, but not serious. Bless her little heart—she was trying her best not to cry, but I could tell that she was already crying on the inside, while being brave on the outside. I kept asking her, "Are you sure you're okay?" I wanted to just give her the opportunity to come and get a reassuring hug in case she needed it. Finally, she broke down and began to cry, and I held out my arms to her as an invitation of comfort. She sat down on my lap, laid her head on my shoulder, and cried out, "I want my mommy!"

Now, at this particular time in my life, I too was in need of comfort. My mom had just passed away five weeks earlier, and I, like this precious little girl, wanted my mommy. I wanted to cry with her, but I knew that if I did, it would frighten the children. I held it in, and mercifully, the moment soon passed for both of us.

There are so many times in our lives when we need to be comforted, but we reject it because the moment comfort comes, so do the tears. We're afraid that once the tears come, they'll never stop. God showed me that comfort brings the tears so that they may wash and heal our souls. If we go uncomforted, the tears might not come, and the pain, anguish, and fear would stay locked inside. Jesus promised before He left this earth to send a "helper" (John 14:16) so that we would not be left alone. The helper is His Holy Spirit and the one who brings us comfort. In those times of sadness, fear, or separation, He uses others to help us unlock that grief. Soon things are better, the world looks a little brighter, and we can go on.

During my grieving period after the death of my mother, I experienced what I would call separation anxiety on a monumental scale. Like the children in preschool who experienced that same kind of distress the first few weeks of school, I needed someone with strong arms and a soft shoulder to comfort me. Just as the teachers and helpers at school comforted the children and helped them adjust to being away from their mommies, Father sent me many comforters to help me adjust and move on. I came to recognize them as my messengers of comfort, and I saw them as a type of earthly angel sent to see me through. It's amazing how Father can take the most devastating of times and bring blessing out of them, just as He used these angels to teach me how to be . . . a messenger of comfort.

Prayer: *Father, You never fail at giving me what I need when I seem to need it the most. I'm thankful I am able to recognize that those many graces have come straight from You, and I'm thankful for those wonderful souls who heard Your voice and obeyed.*

Our Crowning Achievements

*Bless the LORD, O, my soul, and forget not all His benefits: . . .
who redeems your life from destruction, who crowns you with
lovingkindness and tender mercies.*
Psalm 103:2, 4

I think prom-dress shopping is just a dress rehearsal for wedding-dress shopping. It tries the nerves, wears the patience thin, and makes everyone involved emotional, all at the same time. I remember well one such prom-dress shopping excursion, and with disappointment after disappointment, we decided as a last resort to try a bridal shop in hopes of finding something that didn't look like everything else we'd seen that day.

While Sally was busy trying on dresses, I was wandering around the shop looking at all the bridal accessories the store had to offer, when I happened upon a display of beautiful (and expensive) tiaras. I picked up the one that I favored the most and walked back to the dressing room with it. When Sally walked out to show me a dress she had tried on, I placed the tiara on top of her head to see how she would look wearing it. I cannot tell you how much emotion welled up on the inside of me as I crowned my daughter with that exquisite thing. As beautiful as I believe my daughter is under normal circumstances, the tiara appeared to illuminate her, as if the act of placing it upon her head had somehow imparted its very exquisiteness to her. I have to admit that I was so affected in my spirit that I had to fight with everything I had to keep from weeping openly in the middle of that shop (I know—get a grip, Mom!).

What was it that quickened me on the inside so suddenly? While I was waiting for her to try on her other selections, it occurred to me that the Father, who has crowned Jesus the King of Glory, the King of Kings and Lord of Lords, crowns us, His children, as well. The Bible says that He has crowned us with glory and honor (Psalm 8:5), that the prudent are crowned with knowledge (Proverbs 14:18), and that He beautifies, dignifies, and crowns us with loving-kindness and tender mercy (Psalm 103:4). What I experienced as I sat that crown upon my daughter's head was a living picture of what God does for us. Sally's countenance immediately changed as I laid that tiara upon her head. What a change there must be within us when God does the crowning!

Later I looked up the word *crown* in the dictionary, and one of the definitions was "something that imparts splendor, honor, or finish." God imparts Himself into us in order to complete or finish us, and in doing so, we become more like Jesus. These impartations of God into our very beings become our crowns.

You know, I didn't have to chase Sally all over that bridal shop in order to place that tiara on her head. She stood still and allowed me to do so without one single protest. In the same way, we must stand still and allow God to impart Himself and do the work in us that He must in order for us to become as He intended.

You may recall seeing old film footage of Queen Elizabeth at her coronation. As regal and dignified as she looked, she had to humble herself and kneel reverently to receive her crown. We, too, should go to the very throne of almighty God and be still and kneel, humbly awaiting our crowns. No doubt, we will be transformed into something exquisite when we do.

Prayer: *Father, beauty of the earthly kind is fleeting and overrated, but Your beauty, Lord, shines forth on us all forever. Amen.*

Do the Hokey Pokey

The LORD your God in your midst, the Mighty One, will save. He will rejoice over you with gladness, He will quiet you with His love, He will rejoice over you with singing.
Zephaniah 3:17

During my time as a teacher at a Mother's Day Out program, I made it a point to sing with great and enthusiastic regularity "Do the Hokey Pokey." Do you remember it, the little childhood game within a song where you "put your right foot in, put your right foot out, put your right foot in, and shake it all about"? It was especially fun to play it with children who had never met me before; it was a real icebreaker with the little ones. No doubt, it was quite the sight to see me doing the hokey pokey, and I'm positive I wouldn't want to see a video of it. But the children loved it, and it endeared me to them in a way that I'm not so sure I could have achieved so quickly by any other method.

You have to let your hair down to do the hokey pokey and do it well. I've watched shy, reticent children turn into laughing bundles of jelly just from one little round of the hokey pokey. Children who would not speak or maybe even look at me before would grab my knees and shout and giggle with glee at the sight of Mrs. Judy shaking her backside all about. Somehow I became one of them, even though I was most certainly set apart by size and age. They knew, just from that one act of unrestraint, that I was their friend and advocate.

Over the course of every school year, my relationship with the children progressed from that of being strangers to a loving, trusting student-teacher relationship. It was always a transformation that took place outside the safety and nurture of home, which was a first for these young ones. It was always such a pleasure to watch this transformation take place and a privilege to be part of it.

In comparison, when God became a man, He "let His hair down" and became one of us. He laughed and played with the children, befriended people who were unlovable, and taught people who were seemingly unteachable. He endeared Himself to a group of followers who had the privilege of looking into the face of God and sharing in everyday activities with Him. He abandoned His throne and the glory that went with it to become one of us. He knows what it is like to be human—to laugh, to cry, and to be lonely, misunderstood, and rejected. He came into the world and "shook it all about."

Like the experience of my sweet little preschoolers, we change as we get to know our teacher, Jesus, better—we can't help it because the impact He has on us is unlike anything else we ever encounter on this earth, and "that's what it's all about!"

Prayer: *I feel so grateful, Father, for the love of Your little ones and for the way they have always inspired me to be better, to be more like You. I thank You for the example Jesus set while He traveled this earth, shaking things up and loving people in the process. Amen.*

To the Rescue

The LORD will also be a refuge for the oppressed, a refuge in times of trouble. And those who know Your name will put their trust in You: for You, Lord, have not forsaken those who seek You.
Psalm 9:9–10

One stormy day, I was watching the weather news, and the TV station was showing pictures of people in downtown Nashville trying to walk against the wind. Their umbrellas were turning inside out or were being blown completely out of their hands. Full-grown men were having difficulty walking down the sidewalks. I remember thinking to myself that I couldn't imagine walking in a wind that powerful.

Little did I know, that very same blustery day, my daughter, Sally, was experiencing something very similar while at school. Sally is very petite, and her backpack (which probably weighed close to thirty pounds) made walking from class to class a real chore, even in the best of weather conditions. While making her way from one building to another, she found herself caught in the open just as the deluge began. The wind was so fierce that sheets of rain were pelting sideways so forcefully that the water stung her face like a thousand sharp needles, and like a thump from a giant invisible hand, the wind sent her flying to the ground. The weight of her backpack immobilized her, and she was barely able to crawl to a utility pole a few feet away to hang on for dear life.

At that point, Sally realized she was all alone in the courtyard and was terrified that she might very well get caught in the middle of a tornado. All she could do was hug the pole, cry, and pray for relief. And then it came—in the form of a towering mass of solid angelic muscle named Duran, a young man Sally knew from one of her classes. Before Sally could even see who was rescuing her, from his own place of safety he ran out to her, scooped her up (backpack and all), threw her over his shoulder, and ran back for cover. When they reached safety, Sally thanked him profusely. He jokingly reminded her that she needed to "put some meat on those bones" if she was going to walk around by herself in a strong wind.

We've all experienced times in our lives when we needed rescue. That's what God did when He sent a beautiful little innocent baby named Jesus into this cold, stormy world. He rescued all of mankind from a very certain and disastrous future, and in His strength and stability, we are able to walk this earth free from the worry of being blown over by the storms that come our way. We are no longer helpless, because Jesus is our salvation, our strong tower, our refuge, our strength, and our rescuer. A thankful heart remembers the need for that rescue and who it was that got the job done.

Prayer: *Father, I want to always be mindful of the magnitude of what You have done for me. I want to face the storms of life with a thankful heart, knowing that I can always be confident in You. Amen.*

Moving On Up

But we all, with unveiled face, beholding as in a mirror the glory of the Lord, are being transformed into the same image from glory to glory, just as by the Spirit of the Lord.
2 Corinthians 3:18

For her, it was time. At the ripe old age of twenty-one, Sally found a place of her own and moved away from dear old Mom and Dad. She became an independent woman. She had her own car, her own place, her own friends, and her dream career.

Mike and I had mixed feelings. We certainly were very proud of her, and she was happy, healthy, and doing well on her own. We were happy because she was happy, but we had a measure of parental concern, of course. We were completely aware that it's a tough world out there, but we had taught her well. She was (and is) in God's hands, so we tried not to fret too much. She knew that we were there if she needed us. Just because you're a grown-up does not mean that your parents aren't still parents, after all. She had a soft place to fall if she needed to come back home.

I admit that we were a little lonely for her. We missed her. She certainly always brought a spark of life back to the house when she came for a visit or to do laundry. It took time, but we all adjusted. The dynamics of our family life changed. We now had another adult in the family who lived apart from us. We were supportive of her, but now she supported us in many ways too. And that was the biggest adjustment, our attitude towards her. She was no longer just our daughter; she had become a friend.

Some of you who are reading this may not be able to relate. You may still have small children or adolescents at home, and this event may seem so far in the future that you cannot conceive of it. But it will come, and it will come quickly. You need to remember that the whole point of parenting is to teach your children to be independent, productive, and responsible adults, to move out and away and be on their own. Once you adjust, you will be happy about the new living arrangements and the new dynamics. You won't want them to come back because you, too, will enjoy your freedom.

I believe God has similar aspirations for His children. He expects us to grow up in our faith. When we first come to Jesus, we are babes in Christ, but God doesn't want us to stay that way. He wants us to mature, to season and to grow in our trust in Him, to be productive in His kingdom, to sit at the feet of those who know more, and to teach those who know less. He wants us to represent Him. He desires that we know what He has said in His Word and how to utilize that knowledge so that it becomes wisdom in our lives and in the lives of others. The difference in growing up in Him and growing up in the world is that we never have to leave Him the way we grow up and leave our earthly parents. He is always with us, watching us, caring for us, strengthening us, and striving with us, and that can be a great comfort to us all.

I'm very proud of how Sally turned out, for the woman she has become, and it is my hope and prayer that my heavenly Father is proud of me for how I'm turning out too.

Prayer: *Father, thank You for the grace to let my children grow and go, and help me to grow more every day in the image of Your dear Son. Amen.*

Famous Last Words

This is my comfort in my affliction. For Your word has given me life.
Psalm 119:50

Once our children became teenagers, we found ourselves going in different directions more often than together as a family. It was a far cry from the preschool days when if we went out, we all went together and packed the van to the brim with all the necessary accoutrements, whether it was for a two-hour or two-day excursion. And, of course, I could never forget the backbreaking ritual of car-seat placement and buckling. That was something I didn't miss. Those days were gone, and Mike and I, like a set of long-lost grandparents, often found ourselves waving good-bye from the driveway as our children pulled out to go off on adventures on their own.

This began about the time Sally turned thirteen, and we found her leaving the house without us more and more, either to venture off with the families of her friends or in carpooling situations. It was at that particular milestone in her life that my husband, Michael, started a little send-off tradition that continues, for the most part, to this day with both of our children.

As they were leaving the house, he always said, "Have fun, be careful, I love you." It became such a habit that it was almost as if they would hesitate to make sure they heard him say it before they walked out the door. Why? Because it was a blessing from their father. It says so much more than just "have fun, be careful, I love you." It says, "Be blessed in all that you endeavor to do, do the right things that we have taught you, and use the brain that God gave you to preserve yourself, because I love you so much and don't want anything to happen to you." It was a little prayer of sorts, spoken over their sweet little heads as they left our protective custody. I'm thinking that if Sally and Will ever have children of their own, they will be saying to them, "Have fun, be careful, I love you."

Our heavenly Father has spoken these very same sentiments to us over and over again. You can find them between the covers of His Word, the Bible. If we need to feel blessed, reassured, loved, or reminded of His wisdom, we can find it in those precious pages. We need only to look and listen. God's desire for us is to grow to our fullest, to receive His wisdom and apply it to our lives for us to be safe. Why? Because He is a good and perfect Father who wants the best for His children.

The next time you need a special blessing from Him, go on a treasure hunt in your Bible. Very quickly you will find God saying to you, "Have fun" ("Let the saints be joyful in glory," Psalm 149:5); "be careful" ("I will be with him in trouble; I will deliver him and honor him. With long life I will satisfy him, and show him My salvation," Psalm 91:15–16); "I love you" ("And walk in love, as Christ also has loved us and given Himself for us," Ephesians 5:2). So go and be blessed. Have fun, be careful, and remember, He loves you.

Prayer*: Lord, Your words are healing and safety to my soul. Thank You that You always go with me, that You are my delight, and that You are my refuge. Amen.*

Ask the Beasts

Job 12:7–10

A Ladybug in January

*Let heaven and earth praise Him, the seas and
everything that moves in them.*
Psalm 69:34

El Nino is a natural phenomenon that occurs every two to seven years and can have a duration of six to eighteen months. It manifests as a surface warming in the Pacific Ocean and can cause weather patterns to change as a result. The first time I heard of this phenomenon was during its manifestation in the winter of 1997–98, and I remember how many warm days we had that winter and all the talk there was about it.

One of these especially warm days cropped up in January, so we made it a point to get out of the house. It had been cold, and all of a sudden we had spring-like weather. It was one of the most beautiful January days I had ever seen. While we were out and about, I took notice of a ladybug crawling on my windshield. Imagine that, in the dead of winter! I immediately deduced that this must be the result of El Nino, since every shift, change, and peculiarity in the weather that year was blamed on it. Only the weather experts would be able to tell me if this was true.

I'll let you in on a little secret: I know another "El." His name is El Shaddai (God Almighty), and I also know that He is not a natural phenomenon. He is supernatural. He is not worldly at all; He is the living heavenly being who created the universe, the earth, and us and placed within His creation everything we would need. He had no beginning, and He will have no end. He always was and always will be. He is Creator, not created, and He causes all things to be. We can't chalk Him up to an oddity of nature, superstition, or scientific equation. He is because He is.

Spotting a ladybug in the middle of January may be a rare event and even a little treat, a reminder that spring will come again and hopefully soon. But we have a God who walks on the water, stills the storms with a word, and speaks to people from burning bushes. I'm kind of thinking a ladybug in January is not such a big deal, after all!

Prayer: *Father, You are in charge, not the universe, and certainly not the phenomena of this natural world. Help me to remember to place my faith in You and You alone, not the weather or the weatherman, not the scientists, and not the trendsetters or leaders of this age. Amen.*

The Joy of Giving

*Every good gift and every perfect gift is from above, and comes down
from the Father of lights, with whom there is no variation
or shadow of turning.*
James 1:17

It was Christmastime in my third-grade year. Daddy was stationed at Eglin Air Force Base in Florida, and we went home to Nashville for Christmas. I am unsure if I asked for anything in particular that Christmas; if I did, it wasn't significant enough to stick in my memory. But I do know that I got something I didn't ask for.

That Christmas morning, there was a little package that was saved for me to open last. It held four important items: a scrapbook with the title across the front "A Dog's Life," a burgundy leather collar, a photograph of a black-and-tan dachshund puppy, and a note. The note read, "My name is Fritzy, and I can't wait until you come home to meet me."

It took a moment for it to register with me what was going on. I hadn't asked for a dog for Christmas, but the moment I read the note and saw that sweet little baby dog's picture, I was beside myself with glee. My dad, who had hardly been able to contain himself with excitement and anticipation, was crying even before I got the package open.

We spent the rest of Christmas vacation in Nashville, and it was the longest two weeks of my life. Finally, we returned home, and I met my sweet little boy for the first time and fell in love. He was the best and, even to this very day, the most surprising Christmas gift I have ever received.

Throughout our lives, God surprises us with a lot of special gifts that we didn't know we wanted. Some folks end up with children they didn't plan on, or they discover a hidden talent they didn't know they had, or a successful business opportunity lands in their laps when they weren't even looking for one. We just never know what is around the corner. What is important is that we remember where those gifts originate. No matter what we do, we can't outgive God; He is a generous and joyful "gifter." Our heavenly Father loves blessing His children with good gifts—whether we ask for them or not.

Prayer: *I'm not ashamed, Lord, to tell You that I want every blessing You have in store for me. If it is in Your plan, then I know it is good for me, and I will accept it with a thankful heart. Amen.*

Don't Sit on an Egg You Can't Hatch

I, the LORD, search the heart, I test the mind, even to give every man according to his ways, according to the fruit of his doings. As a partridge that broods but does not hatch, so is he who gets riches, but not by right; it will leave him in the midst of his days, and at his end he will be a fool.
Jeremiah 17:10–11

For the most part, we are a dog family, but we have almost always been a bird family too. When Will was a young teenager, we bought him a little baby parakeet, and he named it Boo-Boo. It was a tiny young thing at the time we got it, and it was too early to tell if it was a male or a female. You can never be 100 percent certain; however, I became reasonably sure that Boo-Boo was a female. Of course, my son, being ever loyal to his gender, was in great denial about this. He had wanted a boy bird and refused to acknowledge that "he" very well might be a "she."

Early one morning, Will heard a clamoring in Boo-Boo's cage. He got up to see what was going on and soon came in to inform us, "Uh, Boo-Boo has laid an egg." Over the course of the next several days, she laid two more eggs, proving, of course, that "he" was most definitely a "she." It is amazing how naturally mothering comes to even the simplest of God's little critters, for Boo-Boo quickly became the consummate mother. She shredded the papers in the bottom of her cage, forming a perfect little nest home for her babies, and she became quite protective of her home, watching over the eggs and keeping herself puffed up to look bigger and more ominous to invaders, kidnappers, or other ne'er-do-wells.

Several days after Boo-Boo laid the eggs, I reminded Will that they were obviously unfertilized, since there were no male parakeets in our home. The eggs, if not producing life, would soon deteriorate. In the interest of cleanliness, I suggested that Will remove the eggs to avoid any eventual unpleasantness in his room and ultimately throughout our house. This was tough on Will; he just couldn't force himself to remove those eggs. He knew how proud Boo-Boo was of her progeny—after all, she did think she was going to be a mommy—so I was the one who undertook the task of removing all evidence of Boo-Boo's procreation. I have to admit, though, it was a little tough on me too. I was removing her newfound purpose against her will, and I felt a little sorry for her.

I think many of us can relate to Boo-Boo's predicament. We think we are doing the right thing, something we think we are supposed to do or are called to do, but it just doesn't produce much of anything worthwhile or substantial. We end up devoting a lot of time, focus, and energy to something we should never have undertaken to begin with. Because we don't want to admit we were wrong for undertaking it from the very beginning, we stubbornly stick with it, even after we realize we should give it up.

Life, in essence, is just a series of trial and error, and this is how we learn. We sometimes go the wrong way and make choices that don't have a good outcome. Sometimes we have to lose something we thought we wanted in order to come to the understanding that it was never good for us from the get-go. If we can't let go of it on our own, God finds a way to take it from us. It's His version of tough love. In the long run, however, it works out for the best and for our good. I'm thankful that He watches over us, protects us, and does what is best for us, even if it does rattle our cages once in a while!

Prayer: *Help me, Father, to be watchful and vigilant and to be faithful in seeking Your wisdom concerning all the undertakings of my life. Amen.*

Watch Out for Little Foxes

Catch us the foxes, the little foxes that spoil the vines, for our vines have tender grapes. Song of Solomon 2:15

For Sally's eighteenth birthday, Mike and I bought her a Yorkshire terrier puppy that she named Sugar. This new baby in our house was a two-and-a-half-pound bundle of black- and-tan fur on two-and-a-half-inch legs and was a force to be reckoned with. Every gesture, every look, every gleeful gallop on those tiny legs, and every muffled bark took us off the scale when it came to the "cuteness quotient" and evoked sighs of delight and endless bouts of baby talk from four seemingly adult-type people. All of a sudden, this little ball of "Ewokian" fur took over the household, and someone always had to be watching "the baby."

"Sugie" was too small to jump on or off the furniture, so when she demanded it, we had to be accommodating. Although she had good intentions, not every "tinkle" and "doodle" made it to the newspapers carefully arranged on the floor for her. Like all babies, she didn't sleep all night at first and was given to catnapping at one-to-two-hour intervals between playing, eating, and doing her business on or off the newspapers.

Needless to say, we all had that "there is a new baby in the house" look. Everyone was tired, cranky, and unkempt. The house did not smell all that wonderful either, despite all my efforts with air fresheners and cleaners. There were numerous trips to the vet, the pet store, and the grocery store that were not previously part of our schedule. And yes, of course, we spoiled her. All the things that the puppy manuals tell you not to do, we did them.

Although our world now revolved around this tiny playful parcel of joy, we were attempting to maintain some semblance of normal living, but it was difficult. Dishes had to get done, clothes needed to be washed, and schoolwork had to be completed, but it was not easy. Our family life was no longer running as efficiently as it once had. Isn't it funny how something so small can completely turn your life upside down?

We experience many significant changes and adjustments in this life: times of great joy, great sadness, trial, and testing. But mostly our lives are built on the day-to-day stuff, the little adjustments that we have to make each day that aren't as noticeable in the grand scheme. It's the little things that make up a full life, and it's the little things that can break things down and destroy as well. The Bible calls them "little foxes."

Everyone has suffered hurt feelings, offenses, and misunderstandings. When we choose to leave those offenses unchecked, they can fester, overtake, and consume us, even radically change us—and sometimes permanently. One little misspoken word or mistaken deed not followed by a sincere apology or explanation and the resulting offense can become a bitter resentment in the heart of a person, and harboring unforgiveness will sap us of energy and rob us of quality of life and God's best for us.

Many of us have a little fox or two that we need to take care of today. No matter how great the offense, the power to remove it from our heart begins with our own decision to forgive it, and God then gives us the grace to do the rest. We need to shoo that little fox away before it does some real damage. Things will run more smoothly, and our "houses" will probably smell a little better too.

Prayer: *Father, show me where the little foxes are hiding in my heart, and give me the strength to forgive, forget, and move on. Amen.*

The First Hummingbird Story

I wait for the LORD, my soul waits, and in His word I do hope.
Psalm 130:5

We love our garden and all the wonderful flowers, veggies, and stories it produces. It is an adventure. There is a common theme in learning to live the domesticated outdoor life properly, and that is, like everything else in life, it's all about trial and error.

Mike and I both love hummingbirds. They are unique, and it was our desire to attract them so that we could observe these tiny titans up close and personal. We had always assumed (first mistake) that we could just go to the store, buy a feeder, put it out, and then sit on the porch and wait. After reading up on the subject, we discovered that there were certain types of flowers that attracted hummingbirds, so I stopped reading (second mistake), put down the book, and planted. Then we hung out the feeders and waited . . . and waited. Not a nibble, sip, or sign. Maybe word hadn't gotten out to the hummingbird community that we were in business.

I have to say we should've gotten an A for effort. We kept trying. Year after year, we planted the flowers. Year after year, the special hummingbird food that we had meticulously chosen and purchased at the garden store went into the feeders. Year after year, nothing—no hummingbirds. It was time to pick the book back up and figure out what we were doing wrong. We discovered the key: it was all in the timing. We had been putting out the feeders far too early and then giving up before it was even hummingbird season in our area.

So again we planted the flowers, but we hung empty feeders and decided to be patient. At the end of July, I looked out the front window, and there was a hummingbird hovering in front of an empty feeder. We had a hummingbird customer at the drive-through!

Mike quickly mixed the juice and filled the two feeders on our front porch. Within days, the word was out, and we had an abundance of hummingbirds feasting themselves silly on our front porch. We soon discovered we needed to refill the feeders every few days. Finally— success! I don't know if we were more tickled over the fruits of our labor being realized or just the joy and pleasure that came from watching the birds get their fill of that sweet juice (and arguing with each other over the feeders).

Now, I've always believed God's timing is perfect; but there have been times in my life when I felt I needed action on His part right then, but it still did not come. But His timing *is* perfect, so the problem was with me, not Him. I wasn't ready yet for His answer. I hadn't prepared or checked out the facts and taken care of all my own housekeeping that needed to be done in order to prepare to receive His answer. Obviously, God knows so much more than our little hummingbird friends. He knows exactly when to show up, and we just need to do our part in getting ready for when He does. The waiting grows our faith, and if we allow it, the antic-ipation can be a lot of fun too.

Prayer: *Thank You, Lord, for always being on time. Help me to be patient while I prepare to receive the answers You have for me. Your wisdom and faithfulness are truly matchless. Amen.*

LITTLE PARABLES OF LIFE

A Squirrelly Revelation

If any of you lacks wisdom, let him ask of God, who gives to all liberally and without reproach, and it will be given to him.
James 1:5

I love watching the squirrels on their morning frolics, outrunning our dogs and stealing all the birdseed. They communicate with each other, and they are sneaky, squeaky, and very amusing to me. I realize that many people have negative feelings about squirrels, because like all other wild-life, they are much cuter on the outside where they belong. Little forest creatures quickly lose their appeal when they get loose inside the house, and cute frolicking squirrels are certainly no exception. I learned this lesson myself one day, but it was from a wayward possum that decided to pay us an unwelcome visit.

Will had a friend, Kevin, over for a visit, and they were in the den, playing on the computer. I was working in the kitchen, with the door between the two rooms open, when I heard a disturbance in the den and Will giving a shout of surprise and panic: "There's a possum in here!" I looked around the corner, and sure enough, there was what looked like a possum sitting *on* the desk right next to the computer monitor, watching the engrossed boys playing. Kevin felt differently: "Oooh, I don't think that's a possum!"

A scurry, a scuffle, and a chase ensued. Rather than join in, I quickly slammed the door shut, trapping Will and Kevin in the den with the intruder. (I know—good going, Mom!) I'm a coward, and I freely admit it. I did not relish the fact that there was some kind of critter in my house, but if there was any chance at all of it being a huge rat, well then, these two sixteen-year-old nearly grown men could just fend for themselves. Somehow it escaped, and after two, six, or maybe twelve hours, my heart finally stopped racing, and I let the boys come out of the den.

The intruder was, indeed and thankfully, a possum (for those of you not in the South, "opossum"). With its long tail, pointy face and grasping claws that cling and climb it could easily be mistaken for a gigantic rat, which happens to be a kissing cousin of my little front-yard friends, the squirrels. The next day we discovered a hole in an old dryer vent that led to the crawl space under the house; this had been the point of entrance and escape. Needless to say, it was sealed right then and there for our protection and my sanity.

What you see is not always what you get. What appeals to the eyes and other senses, what tickles the emotions or stimulates the mind and body is subjective and not necessarily what is good for us. Satan doesn't show up at the front door in a red satin cape, sporting a pointy tail and horns to announce his arrival. When evil comes, it is usually appealing and insidious. Discernment is a necessary spiritual gift and a skill that protects us from harmless-looking invaders that can turn our lives upside down.

How can we develop this discernment to protect ourselves and the ones we love? I don't believe there is a pat answer here, but it is has been my experience that patience and prayer are our best tools. Simple wisdom says that if it looks or sounds too good to be true, well . . . you know. If something appears really attractive to me, I have learned not to let myself be persuaded by it without prayer and waiting on the Lord. I often ask for clarity in my prayers, exposure of its true nature, and for discernment and wisdom.

When you are patient and faithful, God will open your eyes so you will know the difference between the nasty rats, pesky possums and playful squirrels of this world. He is trustworthy and I have found that He won't allow you to miss out on something good that He has planned for you, and will never steer you in the wrong direction if you wait on Him to do the revealing and directing.

By learning to wait on the Lord, His discernment will become a guiding strength in your life, and you'll keep the wild things on the outside of your house where they all belong.

Prayer: *Father, I know you are always protecting and guiding me. Open my eyes, and help me to see, not only the evil that comes my way, but the good as well. Amen.*

Jumpin' the Fence

And we desire that each one of you show the same diligence to the full assurance of hope until the end, that you do not become sluggish, but imitate those who through faith and patience inherit the promises.
Hebrews 6:11–12

There's a big old hackberry tree in our yard that is quite the menace. Not only do we track hackberries into the house every day of its season, but there is also a big beautiful doe that is so addicted to them that she jumps over our fence every morning to munch on the berries, much to the chagrin of our two dogs, who don't seem to intimidate her in the least. As the hackberries become less plentiful, she moves on to our tomato garden, much to the chagrin of the humans living at our house, who don't seem in any way able to deter her either.

As annoying as this little scenario is, it also charms us and makes us feel included in a secret life that only the eyes of the forest are generally privileged to witness. It's magical, mystical, "Edenesque." From the doe's view of things, it's just survival: *There is the food. I must go and get it.* She's the ultimate risk taker. She senses the danger and sees evidence of the danger, like my head poking out the doggie door, yelling at her to release my tomatoes. Yet she still goes for it. Full steam ahead—jump the fence. You've got to admire that.

The Bible is full of heroes who took risks. Abraham is one such hero. He pulled up stakes and took his family to a land far away that he had no knowledge of, except that God told him to go there (Genesis 12). David, the little poetic shepherd boy took his sling and ran toward a gigantic enemy and, in one fell swoop, eliminated a menace the entire Hebrew army couldn't touch (1 Samuel 17). And then there's Gideon, one of my favorites. God told him he was a mighty man of valor. He was unsure of himself, but when he obeyed God, he and a mere three hundred men, with God's backing, defeated thousands of Midianites (Judges 6–7).

Faith is a lot like risk taking. Once we become Christians, God expects us to grow and continue to grow in our faith. We do that only by testing ourselves and pushing forward, trusting God and taking risks under His direction. The good stuff, the stuff of the faith life, will feed you, nourish you, and grow you. It is worth the trial, worth the risk—always. It's time to jump the fence. Take some risks. Enjoy the magic. See what the Father is about to do. You'll be glad you did.

Prayer: *Father, I trust in You to open the doors that I am to walk through, and I pray for the strength to continue walking, especially when I can't see what is on the other side. Amen.*

How's Your "Spidey" Sense?

Therefore, my beloved brethren, be steadfast, immovable,
always abounding in the work of the Lord, knowing that
your labor is not in vain in the Lord.
I Corinthians 15:58

It's in the fall of the year when spiders are most plentiful and visible. I'm not a fan and never have been, but I have improved with age. I can tolerate them, and even though my heart rate still increases upon first sighting, I no longer jump, scream, or run away like a manic banshee. And, on occasion, when observing one of the heavenly Father's particularly beautiful versions of this eight-legged wonder, I can appreciate His workmanship . . . from what I consider a safe distance.

In the course of just one week, I experienced the good, the bad, and the ugly of these little creatures. Our sweet dog Arlo was bitten on the leg by a spider, and he was unable to walk for the better part of a day and limped for a full week afterward. A lady I worked with found a spider in a folded pair of pants, a brown recluse meandered across a desk, and an industrious arachnid on the back porch nightly rebuilt his web that stretched across the doorway, after my disdainful and adamant daily demolition first thing every morning.

I guess I have to admire the resilience of the spider. It lives in a land of giants and moves through life without considering the size of the obstacles in its way. The handiwork it leaves in the eaves and corners cannot be equaled by the weavers of the finest Belgian lace. Even when its work is destroyed, it gets right back to work and rebuilds bigger and better than before. It jumps out of the way and rebounds. It doesn't stay down, and it is difficult to destroy. A spider just keeps coming back.

We all need a little "spidey sense," don't we? Life knocks us down. Plans get thwarted. Stuff happens. The real challenge is to keep going, press through, and bounce back. Everyone experiences bad breaks, down times, and hardships. Like the spider, we need to allot no energy to that thing, that giant that caused us to stumble, stop, or interrupted our progress. We need to pick up, move on, and, when necessary, start over. The success is not just in the end result; it's in the resilience and persistence between the start and the finish. So today I will sidestep the giant, keep going, and of course keep my eye out for sticky webs around every corner.

Prayer: *Father, please give me the strength to press through and keep going when life knocks me down. Amen.*

Room for One More

For you are all sons of God through faith in Christ Jesus. . .
And if you are Christ's, then you are Abraham's seed,
and heirs according to the promise.
Galatians 3:26, 29

Our son, Will, has a big heart, especially when it comes to animals; and he has a special way with them as well. One spring afternoon, I picked up Will at school, and when we pulled into the driveway, we noticed a tiny bird, a baby starling, standing on the threshold of our front porch and staring at himself in the reflective glass of the storm door. Will was the first to open the door from the inside and found him still standing in the same spot, mesmerized by his own reflection. He was lost and, we guessed, was looking for someone who looked just like himself.

Needless to say, Will went right to work. Being the "taker in" of all stray animals, within an hour Will had given the baby bird a shoebox home, some worms to eat, and a name: Zeke. Zeke was very scruffy with his fresh, fluffy baby-bird feathers and was very unsteady on his feet. He certainly was not ready to fly just yet. He didn't seem to be injured, but he was definitely a little dazed. The assumption was that he had fallen from a considerable height and lost his way.

Considering Will's substantial emotional investment already, I was sure we were going to have a disaster on our hands if this little bird didn't survive. I let Will keep him on the front porch in his new little home, hoping that he might be able to fly in a day or two. Unfortunately, it was difficult to get him to eat anything from human hands or even from a pair of tweezers, so I became concerned that we were not going to have a successful outcome.

On the third day that Zeke had taken up residence with us, I noticed from the front porch a very active robin's nest high up in one of our trees; the mother and father robin were busily flying to and fro, constantly feeding their three babies. Was it even remotely possible that maybe, just maybe, these good parents would adopt another baby? What was just one more mouth to feed? Reluctantly and carefully, my husband climbed a ladder and placed little Zeke in the nest next to his potential new siblings. I

LITTLE PARABLES OF LIFE

prayed, "Lord, for Will's sake, please give these robins a heart for this poor little ugly duckling of a bird."

We all stood back and watched from a distance. Zeke was much bigger and very awkward- looking in comparison to the baby robins; next to them, he appeared very much out of place. Nonetheless, he seemed to understand the drill. He immediately opened his mouth wide like the others, waiting to be fed. I was so afraid the robins would reject him and push him out of the nest right before our eyes, but we watched, amazed, as incredibly they began feeding that baby starling, just as if he belonged there. We checked every day, and Zeke was thriving and accepted. Several weeks later, he and the others were gone. We knew he'd been able to grow strong enough to fly and strike out on his own.

Many people feel like they don't belong. They have nowhere to turn, and they feel rejected and alone. With God, however, we don't have to be alone—ever. When we accept Jesus Christ as our Lord and Savior, we become adopted into the family of God. The word *adopted* means "placing as a son." We are placed, adopted into His family, with the rights and privileges of an heir to the King and with a citizenship in heaven. I'm willing to bet there is always room for one more, and that's got to be good news for everyone!

Prayer: *No matter where I am in this world, Lord, I have a place called "home" with You. Thank You for making room for one more and accepting me as Your child. Amen.*

No Time for Prudence

But God has chosen the foolish things of the world to put to shame the wise, and God has chosen the weak things of the world to put to shame the things which are mighty.
1 Corinthians 1:27

When Will was a senior in high school, he and a group of his friends went out for lunch one day and found a stray and very pregnant springer spaniel. One of the girls agreed to take her home as long as everyone else agreed to take a puppy when they arrived.

In short order, the dog gave birth to a large litter of puppies. The mother of the girl who had taken in the stray was anxious to have the puppies gone—and quickly—so about five weeks after the birth, the girl stopped by the house with several of the pups so Will could make his choice. It was a heart-wrenching decision, but after about fifteen minutes of back-and-forth between a black one and a brown one, he decided and opted for the black pup, naming him Arlo.

At the time, the family Yorkshire "terror," Sugar (aka Sugie), was three years old and still ruling the roost at our house. She did not appreciate this new infiltrator one bit. Arlo, lonely for his mother and siblings, tried to make friends with her, but she was having none of it and told him so by biting him right on the face. He yelped, of course, and he looked so dejected and heartbroken. Will consoled him the best he could and spent the day holding him and cooing over him, but you could tell that maybe it was just a bit too soon for Arlo to have been taken away from the litter. His loneliness was very obvious, and our hearts were breaking right along with his.

Throughout the night, Will watched over Arlo, took care of him and fed him, but Arlo was a whimpering mess. I wasn't sure what we were going to do about this little sad-sack puppy. The next morning, Will, exhausted and worried, brought Arlo into our bedroom. I lost my mind for a minute and said, "Call her back and tell her to bring that brown puppy back over here." Will's face instantly brightened. He just knew this was going to be a saving grace for Arlo—an expensive one, but one we all hoped would work.

Two hours later, Sunny showed up at our door. Arlo's demeanor instantly changed. They were so happy to see each other. They immediately began exploring the house together, joyous in their brotherly reunion. Throughout those following puppy months, their boundless energy and zeal brought new life to our house and, of course, exhausted us all. They were floppy bundles of fur and vigor, partners in crime, and they spent every minute together. Ten years later, they still do. We always said that Arlo was Will's dog, but Sunny . . . well, he belongs to Arlo. The "boys" are lifelong pals, inseparable hunting buddies, the yin to the other's yang, and they take every opportunity to drive one very ornery, little old lady Yorkie crazy.

Many of us have made decisions based on emotion that didn't turn out well. Impulsiveness can often backfire on us. Of course, it is important to be prudent and wise, thinking things through, praying them through before we act on what we are feeling. However, I also believe God honors loving decisions made in haste, and some of them, I believe, are actually unctions from Him. Should it not be His doing and circumstances don't turn out favorably, He still loves us and gives us the grace for the fallout afterward. If He had to choose, I'm thinking Father would rather us be loving than wise, but our decisions can certainly be both. I'm glad, for Arlo's and our family's sake, that my heart took over and my mind went out the window somewhere, at least for a little while.

Prayer: *Your wisdom and character, Father are unrivaled. Your heart loves the world, and me, and a couple of sweet furry boys who needed a family. Thank You for Your grace that saves us and keeps us, bad decisions and all. Amen.*

Time for a Trim

If you endure chastening, God deals with you as with sons;
for what son is there whom a father does not chasten?
Hebrews 12:7

After the demise of Will's beloved Boo-Boo, we replaced her with two new parakeets at Christmas. The Boo bird had been very tame and could be taken out of her cage. For the most part, she had spent every waking hour on Will's shoulder or chewing up his homework pages. The new birds, however, were not as tame. It is more difficult to tame and train parakeets in pairs; and Will, accustomed to a tame bird, was disappointed that when let out of their cage, the parakeets flew wildly around the house, violently crashing into windows, mirrors, and doors. It was definitely a frustration after his Boo experience.

Clipping parakeets' wings can be an effective practice in taming them, so we did just that, and the little male did great. After his clipping, he immediately took to Will's shoulder and perching on our fingers. He couldn't go anywhere, so he might as well hitch a ride! The female, however, was a different story. Immediately after her wings were clipped, she flung herself to the floor and flopped around until she broke open a blood vessel and began to bleed. No worries—we managed to get it stopped, and she was fine. This pair of birds never did reach the level of tamed domestication as that of the sweet little Boo bird, but they were still a nice addition to the family. They enjoyed each other's company and ours.

In a sense, we have wings too. It's that independent part of us, the residence of our human pride. In our own minds, we might think these wings are essential so we can be free and take flight whenever necessary. But once we belong to God, He will take corrective measures with us the same way we did by clipping our birds' wings. Sometimes He has to clip our wings, trim off some of that pride and independence, to help us understand that He is God, that He is in control and has charge over us. If He didn't, we'd be flopping around foolishly and probably hurting ourselves and maybe others in the process.

If we resist Him, we might bleed, metaphorically speaking. Something that is meant for our good seems like it is painful, yet it was just our own resistance that made it hurt. Almighty God, Creator of heaven and earth, the lover of our souls, always means chastisement to be for our good; He clips our wings so that He can keep us safe and close to Him.

Have you ever been frustrated when you tried to love on your child a little, but he or she wouldn't be still? I know I have. God loves us, and He wants to show us just how much. I think next time I get my wings clipped, I'll be still, let God be God, and let Him show me how much He loves me.

Prayer: *I know from personal experience that it can be exhausting correcting a child. It is a necessary act of love. Forgive me, Father, for my resistance to Your correction, and thank You for loving me enough to stick with it. Amen.*

Open My Eyes

Now faith is the substance of things hoped for, the evidence of things not seen. . . By faith we understand that the worlds were framed by the word of God, so that the things which are seen were not made of things which are visible.
Hebrews 11:1, 3

Do you remember those paintings that were popular back in the day? You know the ones—they were abstracts, and if you focused your eyes at a certain point, then a different picture came into focus. Well, I was never any good at those; I could stand for hours and never get the secondary picture to materialize. It was frustrating. But in a grander way, I learned the trick.

I enjoy my walkabouts in the woods and near the lake when weather permits, and I find the scenery of every season full of hidden treasures and wonder. One wintry day, I found myself on a walk immersed in the monochromatic brownness of the season when I heard a rustling noise and sensed that it wasn't coming from the scamper of squirrels or birds taking flight. It was different, heavier and indiscernible. I was headed downhill, the woods to my right, and continued to move forward but with my head turned toward the woods, keeping a watch for critters of a larger nature that I did not want to disturb.

I kept sensing that I was seeing something, but my eyes couldn't decipher it. Then I saw it. A beautiful and very large doe came into focus not six feet away from me. She was headed up the hill in the opposite direction, and we were parallel, mirrored and face-to-face. We both stopped dead in our tracks; she didn't move a muscle, not a flick of the tail nor a blink of the eye. She seemed confident that I couldn't see her, so I spoke, "I see you." Nothing. She didn't budge or blink. "I see you," I repeated more adamantly. I guess I was expecting her to jump and run away, but instinctively she didn't.

This is where it really gets bizarre. I decided I should move on and took my eyes off her. I looked down and moved forward a few paces, then looked back towards her again, but she had disappeared. There hadn't been a single sound; she had simply and eerily vanished. "Where did you go?" I asked. No response. I scanned the woods and tree line again, but nothing.

I fixated on where I thought she had been before, but she had truly disappeared. I wasn't willing to accept that she had left without a trace or sound, so on a hunch, I kept my eyes trained on that same area and simply backed up those same two paces. She literally materialized before my eyes. She had not moved. She was still watching me, and waiting.

I stood for a moment, marveling at this magnificent creature and how, in His protective and loving care, Father so perfectly fitted her to blend into her surroundings, naturally and efficiently camouflaged. How awesome it was to stand so close to something so ethereal, noble, and instinctively wise. How long she would've stood there, I don't know. I decided there need not be a battle of the wills. I was intruding on her space, after all; I should be the polite guest who didn't wear out my welcome. I took in the sight of her for just a few seconds more and then continued on. I didn't look back again, and I never heard her leave.

I find that when trudging through life, it is easy to miss signs, wonders, and messages from above. They are usually subtle, so it is important to stop for a second and focus. Then Father will make the message plain and clear. Don't miss the signs. Faith is not "seeing is believing." Rather, it is believing *without* seeing. You have to be confident the message is there, watch for the signs, and leave the rest to God. He will most certainly bring it into focus.

Prayer: *Father, I confess that I don't always stop long enough to hear You or even see You in my everyday life, but I am grateful to know that no matter how distracted I am, You are there faithfully waiting to show me You. Amen.*

Returning to the Dirt

Therefore, if anyone is in Christ, he is a new creation; old things have passed away; behold, all things have become new.
2 Corinthians 5:17

Dogs, like people, are peculiar; and though they come in all sizes, colors, breeds, and temperaments, there are certain instinctive and innate behaviors that are common among them all. Now, I do a bit of dog-sitting because I am, after all, a *grandmother* to all dogs. Many folks who entrust the care of their precious *babies* to me would have us believe that their little angels don't know they are dogs and certainly don't act like it. But I would have to differ.

While walking a finicky and very funny shih tzu, I took note that even with all of his breeding and grooming, he was totally fascinated with sniffing trash cans and could not—absolutely could not—resist the temptation to roll in anything dead or some other disgusting object on the ground. Now, the animal behaviorists will tell you that this is most likely an instinct to disguise their own scent so they can hunt prey without detection. That seems valid enough to me. But good grief—a sixty-dollar grooming bill down the drain because you still consider yourself a member of the pack? I guess he was just as irritated at me when I later took away his dignity and gave him a bath; he smelled, once again, like a fancy frou-frou doggie beauty parlor pup instead of the alpha-male leader of the pack he was intended (or hoping) to be.

Again, people aren't much different. How often do we return to old ways that don't make sense, that we know aren't good for us, but we just can't help the fascination? You know what I'm talking about. It came to your mind immediately. It could be a toxic relationship, a bad habit, an obsession with something unhealthy. The list is as long as my arm and as personal as you want to make it. There's an internal struggle to return to the dirt and have a roll-around in it.

The Bible calls this wrestling (or in the South, "wrassling") with the flesh, the "old man" or "sin nature." Heavenly Father made us out of dirt. Jesus was known to scratch in the dirt, and He often made His point with stories of planting and dirt. I'm sure He is quite familiar with our instinctive and very human identification with it. Just as I reacted that day to my little friend's unsavory behavior, I like to think of His grace as a loving leash that He tugs on when we start rolling around in it—a reminder that we are no longer that thing we once were, and that we certainly have Him to rely on, not only to save us, but to keep us clean and smelling good too.

Prayer: *Lord, please help me to resist the temptation to return to old ways and habits that are not good for me. I pray that my attitude and behavior will always be a sweet aroma to You. Amen.*

The Cicadas Are Coming!

Be strong and of good courage, do not fear nor be afraid of them;
for the LORD your God, He is the One who goes with you.
He will not leave you nor forsake you.
Deuteronomy 31:6

I don't know about other parts of the country, but in Tennessee, we have to endure a modern-day plague for a few months every seventeen years: a type of locust that we call cicadas (see-kay'-dahs). One summer after Sally was grown, it was time once again for a two-month visit from these pesky winged critters.

A good friend of Sally's was absolutely terrified of the coming pestilence, so much so that she planned to stay inside for the entire duration of the onslaught of these beady-eyed horrors. The mere mention of the cicadas brought tears to her eyes, and gloom and dread to her core.

Granted, I never look forward to them myself; after all, who wants to hear the unceasing, whirring roar of millions of locusts for several months on end or to have to run to your car every time you go outside just to keep them from flying in your face and sticking to your clothing and hair? It is a major nuisance, and thankfully, we have to put up with it for only a few months every seventeen years.

The only good thing I can say about the cicadas is that at least we know when they are coming. The entomologists can pinpoint almost to the minute when they will emerge, giving us ample opportunity to be at least mentally prepared for them. But unlike with the cicadas, we aren't given a timetable of what is ahead of us in life. There are twists and turns we can't predict or foresee, and we can't stay inside and check out of life to avoid the onslaught that might be coming down the pike.

What we can do is ground ourselves in what is certain in our lives—Jesus—because in Him, we can face the future without fear or dread. It is not necessary to hide ourselves and wait for those irritating nuisances of life to pass. We can face what comes with certainty and confidence because we are hidden in Him, and He has promised to never leave us nor forsake us. Whatever your future brings, I pray that you will know you don't have to face it alone, and that your preparation for all that comes will be rooted in your faith in Jesus.

Prayer: *Life comes, and it comes hard and fast. Lord, I am confident that no matter what my future holds, You will always be with me, strengthening me and walking with me through the good, the bad, and everything in between. Amen.*

Another Hummingbird Story

Show Your marvelous loving kindness by Your right hand,
O You who saves those who trust in You.
Psalm 17:7

One morning during hummingbird season, my husband, Mike, was sitting on the front porch enjoying the unusually cool August weather and reading his newspaper. I was in the kitchen, and I heard him rattle his papers and jump up from his chair. He quickly came into the house and told me, "You'd better come out here! You may never get to see this again!" He grabbed a broom and headed out the door, with me following close behind. There was a bagworm web that had been spun into the outer edge of a large tree near the front eave of our roof, a sure and cunning trap for any small flying creature in a hurry and taking a fast corner around the house.

There he was, a little green-breasted hummingbird, stuck in that sticky mess. His wings were glued fast to the web, and his sweet, shrill little voice called frantically for a welcome rescue from anyone who could help. Mike took the broom and gently stroked the entire web from behind, bringing it down to the ground, with our little friend dangling helplessly in its clutches.

As the web made it to the ground with its helpless little captive, Mike fell to his knees and scooped up the bird. All was still for the next few cautious moments while he straightened the bird's wings and gently pulled away the gooey web. We both crouched down protectively close. The bird, with no other option, lay completely still in the palm of my husband's hand.

Mike looked at me and said, "How many people could ever say they've held such a thing in their hand?" In a few moments, reasonably sure that his little wings were free of debris, we stood on the porch. Mike opened his hand slowly, allowing the hummingbird to take flight when he was ready. At first, he was a bit wobbly, weakened and still a bit sticky, but able to fly, much like a baby bird taking off for the very first time. Away he went, and we were happy and thankful that we had been there to lend him a hand when trouble came.

Life has its traps, its ups and downs, its pitfalls. We've all found ourselves, at one time or another, in sticky messes where we can see no escape, a place in our journey where we are just stuck and paralyzed either emotionally, physically, or spiritually. Avoiding these little traps of life is not realistic; they are part of life. Our maturity shows through when we learn to be wary of these traps. We don't need to be afraid; rather, we can know for sure that when we do find ourselves stuck, we, like our little friend the hummingbird, can trust that we are secure in the Father's hand. If we trust Him enough to be still, He'll clean us up, dust us off, and send us on our way, ready to take on the world and finish what He sent us to do.

Prayer: *Lord, I feel so very grateful and secure, knowing that I am very firmly and most certainly safely planted in the palm of Your hand. Amen.*

Good Things Ahead

For I know the thoughts that I think toward you, says the LORD,
thoughts of peace and not of evil, to give you a future and a hope.
Jeremiah 29:11

I find it very difficult to pack up and go after particularly long dog-sitting visits. If you have dogs, you will have experienced a very natural and typical reaction to the preparations of leaving. They see the suitcases come out and the packing activities commence, and they know they most likely are going to be left behind. And so it begins: the droopy face, the grumbles and whines, the clingy attachment to your leg as you move about the house, and the melancholy resignation found in those big brown eyes.

As I prepared to leave after one such visit, I experienced all of the above and more and kept taking time to reassure my little golden friend, "Daddy will be here soon." He would perk up a bit at the mention of "Daddy," but then continue with his mournful machinations. I kept thinking, *If he could only remember what happened after the last time I packed up to leave, he wouldn't be feeling so blue right now.*

A few hours later, he had his happy ending, and I received a wonderful texted picture with a happy boy on his daddy's lap. All's well that ends well, and I didn't have to feel guilty about leaving him behind, feeling anxious and alone.

Amidst the disappointing and difficult circumstances of life, it's often hard to see past the moment and be positive about the future. We are unable to look ahead through rose-colored glasses, but if we can just take a moment and look back, without much exception we can see that things have almost always worked out for the best. In those uncomfortable times, whether we saw it or not, something better was on its way.

I can't help but think it might be just a bit humorous to God when He sees us anxious, worried, and forlorn, knowing that it is going to turn out really well for us in the end. We have to learn, as we wade through our challenges and difficulties, to accept them as part of life, while knowing all the while that good things, better things, are coming, and Father is the one who is sending them to us.

Prayer: *I often have difficulty being optimistic about things, Lord. Please help me to be mindful that Your plan for me is not only good, but also good for me. Amen.*

The Buzzing in My Ear

Therefore hear me now, my children, and do not depart
from the words of my mouth.
Proverbs 5:7

Commutes to work in the morning are a mundane task of life, and if we are fortunate, uneventful. It is not a healthy thing to disconnect the mind and let the car do the driving on autopilot so that when you arrive at your destination, you have little recollection of the journey. But if you are anything like me, that is probably par for the course. My brain doesn't really seem to turn on until I am seated at my desk, ready for work.

One morning my drive in was a little different. It was a cool morning, so my car windows were down. Shortly after pulling into traffic I noticed (and not so subtly) that a huge wasp was buzzing near my head and was either (a) looking for a place to land or (b) looking for a place to bite. Instinct told me that choice B was the most likely, but since I wasn't comfortable with that possibility, I put on my signal and precariously navigated myself, car and wasp, to the side of the road. Now I'm sure I sound like I was as cool as a cucumber, but I can assure you, this was definitely not the case. I was . . . um . . . loudly and in a very un-Christianlike manner, insulting this wasp and trying my best to find the quickest way to slide out from under his skillful and sinister hover over my head.

Needless to say, I imagine the many passers-by wondered what in the world I was doing when I was finally able to extract myself from the car without getting stung. Then, of course, there was the humiliating wait on the roadside with windows down and doors open for Mr. Accident-Waiting-to-Happen to exit my car.

Now, no worries, I made it safely to work, but I must say that there's nothing like a little buzzing to get you to sit up and pay attention. You know, that little small voice in your gut that quickens you to sit up and take notice, change the route, check the lock on the door, go back and turn the iron off— *that* small voice. It's a pretty good idea to listen to it, heed it, do what it says, follow the unction. That small voice is the Holy Spirit guiding you. It is God's participation in your daily life and is a sign that He not only loves you, but is also watching over you as well. By listening to Him, you can avoid the hassle and humiliations of those "wasps of life" that most certainly will come your way and will most definitely get your attention. Drive safely.

Prayer: *What a blessing it is, Father, that in this natural world, Your voice comes through if we only choose to hear. Help me always to be attuned to Your loving voice and direction. Amen.*

Close Encounters of the Wild Kind

Be sober, be vigilant; because your adversary the devil walks about like
a roaring lion, seeking whom he may devour. Resist him, steadfast in
the faith, knowing that the same sufferings are experienced
by your brotherhood in the world.
1 Peter 5:8–9

In middle Tennessee, many of our neighborhoods, both old and new, have been planted squarely in the middle of woods and farmlands, so whether you live in a suburban or rural setting, there is plenty of wildlife to be seen and experienced. It is not such a rare occurrence to see bats flying in the evening or to hear woodpeckers knocking on nearby trees. An occasional possum may even climb the fence or a tree in the front yard. Barn owls can be seen flying overhead at night, the occasional coyote may wander by, and sometimes at night we might hear the haunting howl of a bobcat.

We were living in an older, more established neighborhood, and my front yard afforded me a view that one might consider uncommon in a suburban setting, given the life and activity that abounded there. One afternoon something quite unexpectedly and forcefully struck the front living-room window.

At first, I thought someone had thrown a rock at the house. I ran to the kitchen window and watched in disbelief as a red-tailed hawk steadied himself and then secured his prey in his talons before his powerful and graceful takeoff. I stood frozen, both in awe of the hawk and in desolation for my little front-yard friend, a squirrel whose life was whisked away swiftly and certainly from the safety of his home.

After collecting my wits, I realized that the hawk must have struck the front window in his descent toward his target. I also realized that as I stared into his eyes from my kitchen, he had been a little dazed from the collision with my window. It took him a moment to center himself with his prey, long enough for me to get a good look at him before he took off with my little front-yard resident, which was now his dinner. As distressing as it was for me, it was also a rare, close-up look at a true wonder of nature.

For the most part, we all live our lives much like this unfortunate squirrel. We work hard, making sure we have enough to eat and a safe place to lay our heads at night. We are aware that there are dangers in the world, but we don't allow those dangers to overwhelm us or prevent us from living life to the fullest. As residents of planet earth, we should, of course, be aware of the dangers of the seen world, but as Christians, there is an unseen world we need to be savvy to as well. There is an evil predator who is seeking to devour us, to kill our joy and our confidence in God and in the power that He has made available to us through Jesus Christ.

Because of Him, we are not powerless; we have authority over the one who would seek to destroy us. We can exercise that power by being aware, by acknowledging the power of God, and by prayer. In exercising our God-given authority, we stun that unseen enemy, making it impossible for him to grab hold of us and carry us away. I thank God that we have His assurance of victory in our everyday lives and that we are safe and secure in His loving care.

Prayer: *The world You gave us, Father, can be a very scary place. But You are mighty, and in You we have a place of refuge and safety. Amen.*

Don't Miss an Opportunity to Fly

Yet in all these things we are more than conquerors
through Him who loved us.
Romans 8:37

On the way home from work one day, I came upon a wild turkey sitting on a fence post near my house. As I rounded the bend, he got a glimpse of me and took flight, up and over my car and into a tree on the other side of the road.

I have to say, two things are noteworthy here (at least, for me). First, I had never seen a wild turkey that close-up before, and secondly, I definitely had never seen one fly. I had always mistakenly thought that turkeys couldn't fly, but it turns out the wild ones can—and it is impressive. It changed my mind about that funny saying "You can't soar with the eagles if you're hanging with the turkeys!" This colorful guy was big, and he lifted his great body with amazing power, enthusiasm, and, yes, grace.

We don't always look like we are suited for any kind of greatness or big achievement, but we can't let the perceptions of others deter us. If you search the Scriptures, you will see that many of those that God made excellent use of didn't seem to be too impressive on their own— Moses, Gideon, and a little virgin girl named Mary, just to name a few. It probably wasn't very evident on the outside, but they had a backup, the same as you and I. You plus God always makes a majority!

Do you spend the better part of your time seizing opportunities and overcoming the odds and the obstacles, despite your limitations? I hope you do. But if not, you are missing out on the privilege of taking part in God's plan. Don't forget that you are on the winning side, and even if you happen to look like a turkey once in a while, just stand back and wait. Soon enough God will have you soaring like an eagle, and if you happen to get a little tired of the struggle, don't worry, He'll make sure you have a soft place to land.

Prayer: *There are many times I feel ill-equipped and ineffective. Help me to remember that it's You who hands me the opportunities and challenges, and it is You who has overcome and conquered them already. I'm just along for the ride. Amen.*

Saying Good-Bye to Lukey-Dog

Be of good courage, and He shall strengthen your heart,
all you who hope in the LORD.
Psalm 31:24

Dog-sitting on occasion is like going on a vacation to me, and spending one-on-one time with the dogs is a great way for me to de-stress and simplify a very hectic life. I do have my favorites, and in their own way, they each teach me about the goodness of God and the beauty of the world. They also not so subtly remind me that I am not the center of the universe, especially at 5:00 a.m. when nature calls us to an impromptu walk outdoors.

This brings me to Luke, aka Lukey-Dog, a magnificent (a word I use often when speaking of Luke) chocolate Lab who departed this earth after a long and glorious life at the lake. There are so many things I could say about Luke that would endear him to you, like how he loved eating car-rots, apples (core, seeds, stem, and all), and doggie ice cream; retrieving a neighbor's newspaper so he could manipulate a reward from you; and being talked to (we all need to feel significant, don't we?). But my favorite memory of him is of our last time together.

Luke was up and out early and being the good old bear he was, he never ventured far from home and could be trusted out on his own. Rather than being efficient with my time that morning, I found myself at a window, watching him savor the day. It was sunny and cool, and the breeze brought in little choppy waves from the lake. Luke was taking it all in: smelling the air as if there were a hamburger on the grill, lifting his face to the sun with a satisfied squint of his old red eyes, and sniffing the ground to follow the trail of a critter that had passed through during the night. He galloped down to the water's edge and took a whiff of lake water, wetting his nose, then rearing his head back to allow the wind to dry it.

He was listening. You could tell the sounds of the lake were like music to him. There were so many delicious sounds coming from so many direc-tions, and I'm sure from far away. He was surveying his kingdom. He was a hunter, a working dog, a companion—and a good one. If you could have given him heaven and all it contained, this is what it would have been like for him. I was awestruck at how alert he was, yet obviously lost in thought, maybe enjoying a memory or two of days gone by, just like an old man on a park bench recalling his glory days. He took one last glance at the lake and trotted to the house, expecting his usual treat. As he turned to come in, something in my soul knew this would be our last time together.

Several weeks later, he was gone. The details don't matter. When an old soldier goes, he just wants to be remembered for his feats of bravery and courage, not for his last struggle. As for me, I'll remember an old-soul face, bear-sized paws, and a heart the size of a mountain. His pet parents called him "the dog of a lifetime." And that's exactly what he was.

I believe that there is a reason God doesn't allow dogs to live as long as humans. If they did, we would never bond to each other; we would just love our dogs instead. He cares for all of His creation, and I believe animals go to heaven. And, I believe that the old Lukey-Dog is there now, on a lake, diving into the water like a two-year-old and swimming straight back with a prize . . . and that Someone is there to reward him with a carrot or two and an apple for a job well done.

Prayer: *Father, You give us the grace we need to live our lives, to brave the trials, and to say good-bye. I am grateful that we never have to say good-bye to You. Amen.*

In the Cool of the Day

Genesis 3:8

The Price of Dirt

And the LORD God formed man of the dust of the ground, and breathed into his nostrils the breath of life; and man became a living being.
Genesis 2:7

My favorite part of spring is when it is time to turn the soil, add fertilizers and new topsoil to my flower gardens, and just dig. I am not a fancy gardener. I don't wear special hats with character or clothes designed just for gardening, and I especially do not like to wear gardener's gloves when I am digging in the dirt. When I dig, I don't use special knee pads or stools to sit on; I practically lie in the dirt itself. I get close to it, spread it around with my hands, and fill my nostrils with the smell of that fresh, wonderful earth. When I come in from digging, I'm usually covered from head to toe with that perfectly delightful dirt. My husband has always said that he knows when his wife is happy. All he has to do is look at the condition of my fingernails. If they're dirty, then I'm a happy girl.

One spring, as I was reclining like Cleopatra in my pile of dirt, carefully spreading it around my newly planted impatiens and thoroughly enjoying myself, I was thinking about the fact that we had visited a local discount store and purchased the very dirt I was squeezing between my fingers. We had actually spent money on dirt. Now, granted, the cost was not much; a forty-pound bag of soil was just a few dollars, but I began to think how silly it was that we had to go and buy it. It was *great* dirt, sure, but you'd think that we should be able to get something so natural and readily available for free (naïve, I know).

The Bible says that God formed man from the dust of the earth (Genesis 2:7). Essentially, He made us out of dirt. Man was nothing more than a mud pie before God breathed His life into that pile of dirt. I find it very interesting that God made us out of something that costs only a few dollars at a discount store, yet He found us to be so valuable that He literally spent the blood of His Son to purchase us back from the devil (Acts 20:28).

It is as if Satan were the owner of a discount store, and God showed up to purchase every last bag of dirt in the place and did so with the most valuable thing He had—His Son. I've always said that Jesus' blood was the most expensive substance in the universe because it was the only thing powerful enough to get us (mankind in its entirety) back where we belong: in the hands of the Gardener who revels in coming closer, experiencing the warmth and savoring the earthy aroma of His creation. I guess dirt isn't so cheap after all.

Prayer: *I am amazed, Father, at how You find worth in me—so much so that You gave Jesus so I might be returned to You, have fellowship with You, and be eternally in Your presence. Father, You are priceless, and because You made me, I guess I am too. Amen.*

The Delicate Balance of Spring

Abhor what is evil. Cling to what is good. Be kindly affectionate to one another with brotherly love, in honor giving preference to one another; not lagging in diligence, fervent in spirit, serving the Lord; rejoicing in hope, patient in tribulation, continuing steadfastly in prayer.
Romans 12:9–12

Ah, the wonders of spring send the senses into overdrive: the thick, intoxicating fragrance of honeysuckle, the busy scamper of little woodland creatures, the sound of boats on the lake and mowers in the fields, frilly pink mimosa blossoms, and the last blooming holdout of the crepe myrtle. Hearts and thoughts turn toward getting a great suntan, planting the vegetable garden, and getting those summer clothes out of storage. Schools will be closing for the summer, so soon our time will be our own once again; and, oh yes, there is the fun of planning summer vacation. Isn't it a great time to be alive?

Then, of course, there is the agony of allergies and hay fever, and water bills going up because the garden needs to be watered on those dry days. Speaking of the garden, there is so much hot, sweaty work required for just a few measly homegrown tomatoes. Those old summer clothes don't fit anymore and are worn-out—and my arms look so flabby in those sleeveless summer shirts. The kids get bored and drive us crazy after one week of no school. Why can't they just go outside and play? Summer camp is a good option, but the cost is astronomical. For the same reason, forget summer vacation. We can't afford it. We'll have to do a "staycation" instead—again.

For some folks, the glass is always half full. Then for others, it's half empty. The fact is, there is only so much water in that glass, no matter how you look at it. It's what you make of it that counts. There is a balance to life. There is never a shortage of things to look forward to and enjoy, but then there is always a downside to most things as well. Sometimes optimism can be a denial of the way things truly are; and pessimism, a jaded lack of faith.

It's important that we be positive, forward thinking, and uplifting, but not be so heavenly minded that we are no earthly good. Christian maturity is best represented in those who have their feet firmly planted on the earth and grounded in the Word, while consistently looking upward and being hopeful. It's a balance. It's what makes us the salt of the earth. Seek that balance and Father will surely see to it that you get it. No matter how you look at it, there will be plenty of water to go around for everyone!

Prayer: *I know who my source is, and I thank You that no matter the condition of my outlook, You are still You. I can count on You to balance it all out and keep me straight. Amen.*

Sowing the Good Seeds

Death and life are in the power of the tongue,
and those who love it will eat its fruit.
Proverbs 18:21

In our neck of the woods, there is no lack of mature silver maple trees. Each spring, they develop these little seedpods that in the course of a week are released by the trees and the wind and sail to the ground, twirling like the blades of a helicopter. When they are released, there are literally millions of them that can be seen twirling and winding their way through the air and down to the ground. It is quite a sight to behold. There are so many that it's reminiscent of a swarm of insects like locusts.

After a few days, little maple tree seedlings start popping up everywhere. They are in my gardens, my potted plants, the cracks of the driveway, and even in my rain gutters on the house. As late as August, I can still find these little seedlings that catch hold of the ground, take on a little water, and then sprout. The seeds certainly do their job.

The Bible says that the Word of God is like seed, and the sower (planter) sows (plants) the Word (Mark 4:14). As imitators of Christ, we also can sow our words into others. When raising our children, it is so important that they hear words of truth, loving-kindness, and encouragement from us, words that will take root and grow them into honest, loving encouragers. If they hear words of anger and disappointment, however, those words also can take root and grow them into angry, bitter people.

The same is true for adults as well. There are people you encounter every day who need to hear encouragement and good words, and it may be that God is the one who sent you to do it. What a blessing it is to see someone respond to "Good job!" "You were great!" or "I'm proud of you!" I discovered very quickly as a counselor that even my oldest clients responded positively to these affirmations. These words of encouragement produce a fruitful crop.

We have an awesome responsibility to represent Father well as we walk this planet—to be His voice and sow loving, Jesus-filled words into the lives of others so that they will be blessed, grow, and eventually sow those good seeds into the people that they encounter. That's what seeds do:

they reproduce and grow plentiful crops year after year. Let's make sure we are sowing the good ones.

Prayer: *Please help me to remember that there is power in the words I speak, Father. May I always speak words that speak well of You. Amen.*

Little Legacies

As for man, his days are like grass; as a flower of the field, so he flourishes. For the wind passes over it, and it is gone, and its place remembers it no more.
Psalm 103:15–16

Children are full of questions. I remember my daughter, Sally, asking me once, "Mama, what's your favorite sound in the whole world?" My answer then was the same as it is today. I have two favorite sounds, and the first was the sound of my children laughing— you know, those carefree belly laughs they have when they are little. There is no better sound in the world; it sparks instantaneous joy in the heart of a mother. Second, I love to hear the wind in the trees. When the seasons change, especially from winter to spring and from summer to fall, there is a lot of wind bringing in those changes. I love to sit and listen to the sound and watch the whipping of the branches and the reaction of the leaves to the movement of air around them. To me, that's the best sound in nature. Hearing those powerful gusts brings much peace to me.

I think God reveals His own nature a bit in the wind. It is gentle enough to make a quiet clatter and reveals its existence without actually being seen. Father, too, is gentle with us. He moves us, and it is obvious we are being moved. It is a beautiful and splendid thing to be moved and used by God. He reveals Himself to us in the most delicate of ways, like through our children's laughter or that feeling we get when we know we have just blessed someone. We don't actually physically see Him, but we just know that He's there by what we've experienced.

The Bible says that our lives are like the grass and the flowers: we grow, we bloom, the wind passes over us, and then we're gone. Our lives are but a season compared to eternity. I want to make my season count. I want to leave a legacy of love and joy. I hope my children remember that I loved to hear them laugh and enjoyed the sound of the wind in the trees and the wind chimes in the garden, that I delighted in the vision of a butterfly lighting on one of the flowers I had planted, that I saw God in everything.

Are you enjoying your days with the sun in your face and the wind in your hair, listening for those sounds that give you peace? I hope so. Life is short, and there is no time like the present to leave a little legacy or two.

Prayer: *Your legacy to me, Father, is Jesus. May I never take for granted the grand and wonderful thing You have done, and may I treasure it as much as any of the lovely moments You have generously given me in my season here on earth. Amen.*

Counting On the Seasons

God is not a man, that He should lie, nor a son of man, that He should repent. Has He said, and will He not do? Or has He spoken, and will He not make it good?
Numbers 23:19

On my way to work one spring morning, I noticed a forsythia bush that had already dropped all its blooms. A somber, but brilliant puddle of yellow surrounded it on the muddy ground. It occurred to me that the blooming season seemed to have been abbreviated a bit. No doubt, we had endured an extremely cold winter with several deep freezes and snow, followed by many early spring storms, and I felt that maybe these weather extremes were the culprit. Redbuds, Bradford pears, tulip trees— they all looked a little haggard for this time of year. It was sad for me, as I am energized and motivated by the glorious spring colors, especially after a long, hard winter.

God has promised us in His Word that the seasons will carry on; seedtime and harvest will continue (Genesis 8:22). He set it all in motion, and until He tells it to stop, it will keep happening. Even with climate changes and extremes, and a resulting abbreviated season, it is good to know that it is something we can count on.

This reminds me that Father is consistent. *He is not a man that He should lie.* What He says, He does. It is His integrity, and it is reliable. When I look into His Word, I can find the revelation of His character. I can know what to expect from Him, and He certainly knows what to expect from me. I'm not anywhere nearly as reliable as He is. I'm human. I have lied, I have messed up, and I have not followed through. But He is faithful to forgive me and to help me become more reliable.

We are promised that there will always be at least some semblance of seasons, and the earth will prove that we can count on it. I am so glad that Father is someone I can count on, and my hope is to be someone that He can count on too.

Prayer: *Father, thank You that I know what to expect from You and that I am never disappointed. Amen.*

The God Kind of Love

For the love of Christ compels us, because we judge thus: that if One died for all, then all died; and He died for all, that those who live should live no longer for themselves, but for Him who died for them and rose again.
2 Corinthians 5:14–15

I wanted some rosebushes for my birthday. Mike's grandfather, G-John, was married to a lady, Betty, who had spent a lot of years growing beautiful roses, and I had been an admirer of them for quite some time. When they asked me what I wanted for my birthday, I told them I thought it would be nice to have a few rosebushes for the garden in front of my living-room window.

I had no idea this was going to become a very complicated and labor-intensive process, one that was going to be very costly to my husband—and I don't mean in dollars. On my birthday, G-John and Betty showed up at our house with the trunk and backseat of their car filled to the brim. She had previously asked Mike to dig up the garden ahead of time for three rosebushes, and he had done just that—he thought.

Immediately, she began barking orders with the skill of a drill sergeant and told Mike that he was going to have to dig deeper and wider to make plenty of room for the bushes. For the next two hours, he obediently dug a hole that made the neighbors think we were preparing for a burial. Drenched in sweat and ready to collapse, he then was given very specific instructions on phase two of The Great Birthday Rose Project.

He was directed to unload several large, *very* large bags of soil, compost, lime, and some other fancy dirt-type stuff that to this day I have no idea what it was. He had to take shovels full of each of these components and mix them together in a wheelbarrow and then dump it into the "abyss" and repeat this process until the rose bed was a little over half full. Only then was it finally time to add the rosebushes, which he did, precisely to all the verbal specifications. Finally, he filled in the hole with more mixture and then mulched on top of that. In total, I think this was somewhere around a six-hour operation, including the first digging he had already done.

The rosebushes were nice, beautiful, and, I'm sure, very expensive. I was thankful for the gift; the proper thank-you note was sent. We enjoyed and took care of them for the better part of a decade, but now I can't even be positive what color they were. What has always stuck in my mind, the part that was most endearing and appreciated, was my husband's hard work and sacrifice to plant them. The beautiful blooms eventually went away, but not the memory of his loving labor (and submitted humiliation, for certain).

Love, the God kind of love (*agape* love), is demonstrative. It compelled Christ to the cross and held Him there after the scourging and the bleeding and throughout the messy excruciating labor of giving His life for all mankind. It is a privilege to be on the receiving end of this kind of love. We didn't earn it. We didn't deserve it. And we could have never done it for ourselves. The only appropriate response is that the way we live out our lives should be nothing less than a living, breathing "thank you" to God for what He has done for us.

Prayer: *I'm grateful Father, that You gave me a husband who shows his love for me in such beautiful and selfless ways. Even more so, how grateful I am for what You have done for all of mankind. It is my prayer that I am always mindfully thankful and tell You so every day. Amen.*

A Morning Glory Tale

My eyes shall be on the faithful of the land,
that they may dwell with Me.
Psalm 101:6

I love the morning glory. It's a hardy, romantic, and old-fashioned sort of trumpet-shaped flower that grows on a vine. Its brilliant blooms open in the morning and close back up in the evening, thus the name *morning glory*. Oh—and did I mention?—I love them.

One year in particular, I had a bountiful crop of these beauties. The vines and blooms were so dense that the wear and tear was quite extensive on my trellis. The next year, it was obvious the trellis had seen better days; it was rotted and bowed, so we had to tear it down. My intention was to put up a new trellis or some kind of support for the enthusiastic climbers to grow on. Despite my good intentions, when spring came around, I was busy with work, school, and other activities, and I ended up not putting up a new trellis, thus missing the opportunity to plant any new morning glory seeds.

Before long, it was obvious that the resilient little morning glories had other intentions, despite my neglect. The annual beauties from the previous year had reseeded themselves, and by midsummer I had heart-shaped leaves all over my garden. They were climbing on taller plants, shepherd's hooks, and other garden knickknacks—they were everywhere. And, of course, they were incredibly beautiful: brilliant fuchsias and royal purples, periwinkle blues and delicate pinks.

I certainly couldn't take credit for the splendor of this section of my garden. I had done absolutely nothing to grow them. They had come up and established themselves on their own. There was no point in being proud of my gardening abilities; the flowers certainly didn't need me.

After about a month of the morning glories spreading throughout and blooming everywhere, I realized a little intervention was necessary. They were taking over and choking out my other plants. I broke off some of the vines and placed them on Mike's burn pile. The vines I removed had several bold flowers on them, and I noticed for several days thereafter that even though the vines had been torn away from their roots, the blooms were still opening every morning. I counted five full days in the summer heat with no water source, and they were still beautiful and opening every morning. That is real resilience.

Like my morning glories, but so much more so, we need to be persistent. However, we're not on our own; we don't have to find ourselves torn away and removed from our Source. When we remain rooted in Him, Father God endows us with the strength we need to persevere. He is a much better gardener than I am, thank goodness. He will water us with His Word and won't neglect us as we grow. I believe it makes Him happy to see us thriving and blooming. He admires what He has done in His creation, and unlike my poor morning glories, we are never discarded or abandoned, only nurtured and watched over.

You are His brilliant creation, a masterpiece so much greater than a morning glory. And that's a great motivation to be faithful and to persist.

Prayer: *Please forgive me, Lord, for my lack of tenaciousness, for those times when I get lazy, unfocused, and unmotivated. Thank You for Your gentle encouragement and loving inspiration to persist and to get down to business. Amen.*

The Beauty of Mercy

Praise the LORD! Oh, give thanks to the LORD, for He is good!
For His mercy endures forever.
Psalm 106:1

One year I made the mistake of planting my morning glories on a side of the house where I didn't have a good view from any window. I couldn't enjoy them from inside in the morning, which is when the blossoms are open and magnificent. One day I got up a little earlier than usual and walked outside and around the corner of the house to enjoy my garden. There they were—open and splayed out, a gorgeous sight and eye candy for sure. It occurred to me that it wasn't the location or the flowers that had been inaccessible, but rather, I was not making myself available to enjoy my favorite flowers every day.

The Bible says many things about mercy, but two of them initially sound contradictory to one another: His mercies are new every morning (Lamentations 3:22–23), and "His mercy endures forever" (Psalm 106:1). How could it be that something that goes on forever could be new every day? The story of my morning glories gave me the answer to the riddle. It's about how we receive God's mercy. We can depend on it forever, because He is faithful and true, but we are in need of a fresh dose of it every day. My morning glories are blooming every morning, but unless I take the time to go out and access their beauty, they do me no good.

Are you in need of a fresh dose of mercy? Do you maybe need to extend it to someone else? I think you will find that when you do, you'll be on the receiving end of a good deal of it yourself. Thankfully, Father always has a fresh dose of it for us every day. We just need to peek around the corner and take it all in.

Prayer: *Thank You, Father, for Your mercy. I pray I will be a reflection of Your mercy to everyone I encounter and that You may be glorified because of it. Amen.*

Toil and Trouble

For I know that my Redeemer lives, and He shall stand at last on the earth.
Job 19:25

It was a hard year in the garden. Mike found himself more dedicated than ever as a weekend farmer to give it what it needed and to produce a bountiful crop. We planted five kinds of peppers, four varieties of tomatoes, summer squash, cantaloupe, and herbs.

The weather was erratic, with too much rain, then a drought. The spring temperatures did not increase gradually but rather turned from freezing to sweltering overnight. It really wasn't a spring at all; we progressed from winter to summer in just a matter of days.

We continued to learn and ask a lot of questions. We read a lot of articles on the Internet, talked to the experts, and then put into practice our newfound knowledge. It was that old trial and error all over again. Our veggies didn't do very well. The squash had a good run in the beginning but then just petered out by July 4. The cantaloupe . . . well, we made all kinds of mistakes with it, and we never got a single one. Only one pepper plant produced anything noteworthy. The tomatoes stayed green for far too long; then the fruit would split and become bug and groundhog food. While we did get a small crop of tomatoes a bit late, they were not the yummy treats we had come to know and love. It was disappointing, but that's gardening.

This kind of disappointment should be no surprise to us. The Scriptures say, "Cursed is the ground for your sake; in toil you shall eat of it all the days of your life" (Genesis 3:17). Then why keep trying? Well, for one, we've got to eat. But more importantly, it shows our faith. In hope, we fight and struggle against the elements and the other forces beyond our control, and it makes us stronger.

God cursed the ground because of Adam's disobedience, but before He pronounced this verdict over Adam, in His very typical fashion He gave us a promise we could hold on to, one that would keep us going in the tough times. Just back up a few verses and you will see it. In cursing Satan, He showed us the future: "And I will put enmity between you and the woman, and between your seed and her Seed; He shall bruise your head and you shall bruise His heel" (Genesis 3:15). That was great news: a Savior would surely come; our redemption was already planned!

In spite of our struggles throughout life, Jesus will always be our good news. The curse, evidently, is still in effect on the ground, but the Seed on the inside of us has redeemed us from the curse and is more than able to produce a really good crop.

Prayer: *I love how You teach me in the garden, Lord. Because of Jesus, I can look forward to a perfect garden to tend to in heaven, where there will never be a shortage of good fruit or good lessons from my heavenly Father. Amen.*

The Farmer's Helpers

*Do not be deceived, God is not mocked; for whatever
a man sows, that he will also reap.*
Galatians 6:7

My husband and I truly enjoy observing wildlife. It is one of our favorite pastimes to sit outside and watch the animals eat, drink, make homes, raise babies, and enjoy their lives. I imagine our annual investment in birdseed and dried corn for the squirrels is substantial; I've decided I'll just stay in denial about the actual figure. On most days, as many as six squirrels, several bunnies, and scores of different types of birds, including cardinals, bluebirds, blue jays, nuthatches, finches, and of course blackbirds horning in on the others, are visible in our yard. If we sit still and stay quiet (and lock the dogs inside), the birds will feed within several feet of us. It is rewarding and peaceful.

We were having difficulty keeping the squirrels off the bird feeders, a common problem. The seed was spilling all over the ground, and some of the birds wouldn't go to the ground to have their dinner. We tried several types of feeders that aren't supposed to be squirrel friendly, but squirrels are industrious and clever, and the new feeders never worked out. We decided that we couldn't beat them, so we joined them and started buying dried corn just for them. That made us all happier campers.

One day I noticed a squirrel pulling single grains of corn off the feeder, sliding down the tree with the corn in his mouth, and then burying it in the yard. He repeated this procedure many times until the better part of the entire ear of corn was gone. He was very smart, efficient, determined, and—I have to say it—cute. I came to the conclusion that he must be storing food for the winter, but I couldn't imagine that the corn wouldn't deteriorate before he could access it when he needed it. Of course, I was forgetting one important fact: grains of corn are seeds.

I didn't give this little scenario another thought until one day I noticed a funny-looking weed in my large planting pot in the front garden. After closer inspection, I realized it looked like a stalk of corn. I carefully weeded it out of the pot, and when I had pulled it out completely, lo and behold, there was a grain of corn at the root where it had sprouted. Those little stinkers were growing corn in my flower garden! Before long, we began to notice lots of little corn plants throughout the yard. As an experiment, we decided to leave one growing in an out-of-the-way place to see if it would actually produce corn by fall. We watered it and watched as it grew from a little sprout to a knee-high cornstalk.

I have to interject here that in my years of gardening, I have experienced both success and failure. No matter my apparent consistency or expertise, sometimes it seems like it is just the luck of the draw as to whether I will have a garden that produces well. However, I do pride myself in doing fairly well as a gardener, but now here were these little critters planting corn with their little squirrelly paws, not noting the location, sunlight, water, or soil pH, and growing a plentiful cornfield in my yard. I knew, of course, this was just their instinct, but the outcome was still the same. The end of the story is, yes, we had a small harvest of "squirrel corn" that year from the one plant that we allowed to remain.

God thought this up. In His wisdom and vision in creation, He devised His principle of sowing and reaping, seedtime and harvest. We can plant the seed, water it, and harvest it, but it is because He set this in motion from the foundation of the world that it works. Anyone can plant a seed, but it is God who causes it to grow.

Whether we are planting a garden, investing in our marriages or other relationships, raising our children, sharing our resources, or serving God, this principle is in effect. We have to do our part, which is to sow, and He does the rest. I want to plant something every day. I want to water it, then watch and see what remarkable thing Father does with it.

Prayer: *I thank You for Your seed principle, Lord. I feel privileged to be able to take part in the work of Your kingdom by simply sowing. I ask for opportunities every day. Amen.*

Lord, Give Me Impatiens

Therefore submit to God. Resist the devil and he will flee from you.
James 4:7

As you may have gathered, we've got critters—wild ones, tame ones, and everything in between. Some are welcome, but then some are not. Our dogs, Arlo and Sunny, are hunters. They chase squirrels and flush birds and deer from the thickets. Arlo loves box turtles; he sniffs them out and then picks them up and carries them for miles. He doesn't know what to do with them once he gets them in his mouth, but they are trophies nonetheless. Arlo (and we) have had to suffer through the aftereffects of chasing a skunk, and he has been known to bring a dead mole or two and a dead bunny through the doggie door. Sunny, for the most part, is the point man, and Arlo is the one who moves in and seals the deal. There certainly can be a downside to living with and around animals.

Here is what is interesting, among other things, about our dogs. I'm pretty sure Arlo has learned his lesson when it comes to skunks, but both he and Sunny are obsessed with the unfortunate toads that happen through our backyard. They will smell one, pinpoint its location, and promptly send it to its most ill-fated demise . . . *every time*. These toads emit a type of toxin through their skin that causes a reaction in the dogs, and they commence shaking their heads and drooling uncontrollably after they have encountered one. These uncomfortable side effects last for about half an hour afterward, but the dogs continue to hunt and kill the toads and experience this same reaction . . . *every time*.

You are probably saying to yourself by now that this is not a gardening story, but it is. There is a tree in the backyard that these toads are particularly drawn to, and we planted some hostas at its base. In their feverish and enthusiastic amphibian hunting, the "boys" were digging up the hostas. Mike decided to try and save the plants by building a garden around the hostas; he put up a barrier fence and filled the area with the most beautiful and brilliantly colored shade-loving impatiens—one of my favorites—and ironically, a little garden statue that looked like a giant mushroom with a sign on it that said "Wart-mart."

The flowers flourished and filled the garden throughout the summer with amazing color, and the dogs, for the better part of the season, stayed away. It was an act of genius . . . well, almost. Eventually the temptation became too great. I guess a few toads too many had invaded the garden, and the boys . . . well, you can assume the rest. The impatiens garden was no more.

Dogs, being the animals they are, are driven by instinct. They can't help themselves. We, too, have natural instincts and the will to survive, but as humans, reason (and sometimes obsession and compulsion) rules our thinking and actions. After we become Christians, we are still not immune to temptation. The toads will wander in. We can put in a flower bed and surround it with a fence in an effort to pretty it up, but we will never stop being tempted.

God understands. He's been there, done that. Jesus was tempted. He understands the dilemma of it, but the excuse "the devil made me do it" doesn't work anymore. He has delivered us from the law of sin and death and given us His Holy Spirit to help us. We have the power—His power—within us to resist. It's up to us to choose to act or not to act when we are tempted . . . *every time.*

Prayer: *Thank You, Father, for Your provision and the strength to resist temptation, and for Your sufficient grace when I don't. Amen.*

A Tree Among the Rubble

The righteous shall flourish like a palm tree. He shall grow like a cedar in Lebanon. Those who are planted in the house of the LORD shall flourish in the courts of our God. They shall still bear fruit in old age; they shall be fresh and flourishing, to declare that the LORD is upright; He is my rock, and there is no unrighteousness in Him.
Psalm 92:12–15

We used to pass a vacant lot every Sunday on the way to church. Formerly, there had been a doctor's office and a pharmacy at this location, but the building was long gone. All that was left was a wasteland of rock and debris from the demolition of the building, piled up behind a chain-link fence.

During the spring prior to 9-11, I took notice of a magnolia tree standing in the very center of the lot, surrounded by rocks, dirt, and weeds. It was blooming at the time, covered with huge, white, leathery blossoms and looking very much out of place there. The tree had not reached full maturity, but it was a fairly good size, thriving, flowering, and peeking out from behind the giant debris piles. I'd never noticed it before, yet there it was, humbly blooming in the midst of that abandoned wasteland.

Later that summer, on 9-11, as I watched in horror the attacks on New York City and Washington, D.C. and the ensuing aftermath, the rubble remnant of what had once been the World Trade Center reminded me of that little vacant lot and the tree in its center. All that was visible that day was the horrible destruction and the "little trees" working in the midst of it, struggling so hard to overcome it.

Like that tree, we don't always grow because of our circumstances—we grow *in spite* of them. It doesn't necessarily have to matter where we are planted, whether it is a peaceful green meadow or a pile of rocks and dirt. All that is needed are firmly established roots, the sun, and the rain in order to continue to grow and bloom. The hardships seem to enhance the growth, and the aesthetics certainly don't matter.

As we come out on the other side of the trials and tests of this life, often all that seems to be left behind are the ruins and the stronger, more determined tree standing in its midst. We find we've grown; with firmly established roots in the Lord, our peace and strength are *increased in* Him,

114

our fear and dread have been *decreased* by Him, and our resolve to keep flourishing is *multiplied* through Him. The result is we continue to grow stronger, upward and away from the rubble at our feet, weathering and welcoming the rain, our faces turned toward the Son. We bloom where we are planted. We thrive, survive, and overcome.

The last time I passed my little magnolia tree, I noticed something new. There was a billboard towering over the lot that I had not noticed before. Upon it, these words were written: "In God We Trust, United We Stand."

What a fitting tribute to a tree that stands among the rubble. Be strong in the Lord.

Prayer: *Father, in Your house, I flourish and You strengthen me. I thank You that I do not have to fear what the future holds because You are mighty, always faithful, and Your love never fails. Amen.*

Where's the Water Fountain?

But whoever drinks of the water that I shall give him will never thirst. But the water that I shall give him will become in him a fountain of water, springing up into everlasting life.
John 4:14

I had a plant that I kept on my bathroom counter: a pothos, a great starter plant for the novice, needing very little expertise. They require very little water, do fine without much light, and don't care if they have three inches of dust or if you shine their leaves every week. Fertilizer . . . what's that? In fact, the only time I ever gave much thought to the poor thing was when I got out of the shower in the mornings. Once I left the bathroom, it was "out of sight, out of mind."

One day I noticed that it was looking a little wilted, a little shriveled, not completely healthy. It was still green, and its vine was still wrapped around my towel rack; but it had lost some of its luster. If it were a person, I'd say it looked sad, maybe even depressed. Although it was alive, it was not functioning the way it should. That's when the thought struck me that I didn't remember when I had watered it last, and that it may have been as long as six weeks. In fact, I couldn't remember the last time that I had given it any physical attention at all. I looked at it every morning, but I hadn't done anything to maintain or care for it. No wonder it looked depressed! The irony of it all is that it sat less than a foot—twelve measly inches—from my bathroom sink, a water source.

Our souls are very much like that plant. It is remarkable how we can get by, day in and day out, with very little attention to our inner man. But in the end, just getting by isn't really good enough, not if we are to truly be vibrant children of God, the "kingdom kids" He expects us to be. Lack of attention to our spiritual needs can lead to depression, emptiness, a lackluster life, and a sense of "is this all there is?" We can become jaded in our thoughts and attitudes in matters of faith. It doesn't speak well of our ambassadorship to the world.

For our physical well-being, we require the right kind of food, water, exercise, and fresh air to feel well. For our inner well-being, we require feeding and watering of a different kind: time reading and meditating on the Word of God.

Most of my Christian life, I have carried a Bible with me wherever I went, a pocket one or even my regular study Bible. At the very least, I have kept one on the backseat of my car. These days, with the Internet and cell phones, we have access to the Word of God 24-7, 365 days a year. Without exception, we have access to it constantly, if we want it. I'm sure for all of us, it is never more than a mere few feet away.

But unless we take the time to access it and absorb what God has for our souls to feed on and be nourished by, that Bible does us no good at all. It's just like the plant sitting by the bathroom sink yet getting no water; after a while, the inattention will take its toll on us. Little by little, we will become less vibrant, less enthusiastic, less alive.

Isn't it a blessing to have a tangible love letter from Father that reveals who He is, tells us how much He loves us, and teaches us how to experience life in a much fuller, more joyful way? I want to drink Him in through His Word. How about you? Are you thirsty? God's water fountain never runs dry.

Prayer: *I am so grateful for Your Word, Father. It and You have never failed me, and I pray that my meditations upon it are acceptable to You. Amen.*

Summer's Fading Beauty

Charm is deceitful and beauty is passing, but a woman
who fears the LORD, she shall be praised.
Proverbs 31:30

I was deadheading my much-neglected (and for you gardeners out there, very "leggy") petunias one morning, and with a nostalgic sigh, I realized they didn't have a lot of time left before they would be replaced with some fall mums. Their brilliant and glorious turn at my front-porch beautification project would soon be over. After a little trimming, plucking, and watering, however, those petunias got perky. They stood a little taller and looked brighter, rejuvenated. I told them, "You are still beautiful, after all."

I was immediately reminded that on a lot of days, I feel like those petunias—past my prime, a little worse for wear, too much time in the sun and not enough pampering. On the inside, I still feel like that young, fresh, and blossoming girl, but with my first look in the mirror in the morning, I am shocked to see someone else staring back at me. Upon closer scrutiny, I can still see the young girl there. Behind the eyes, she is still there; she just knows more now.

Wisdom is the application of knowledge. It's not enough just to learn something; you have to live it too. Learning should never end, especially in the faith life, and I have discovered that with experience hopefully comes wisdom. I don't want to turn back the clock, get a face-lift, or become naïve again. I like knowing and living what I know, not having to relearn the same lessons all over again. God is faithful to train us and mature us, and when we are actively involved in that process, the learning and application are very rewarding.

Summer had come and almost gone, and with it, some of its beauty had faded. However, upon closer inspection, I could see that the lake still sparkled with flashes of sunlight. The flowers were still vibrant, albeit a bit wilted. The crickets still chirped with relish amid the early morning dew, and the hummingbirds were still partaking of the sweetness of life. I daresay that fading beauty has its own particular charm and character. Whether it's the fading beauty of a beloved time, thing, or person, there is still plenty to appreciate and enjoy. It was not yet time for me to give up. Summer had a little life left in her, and thankfully, so did I.

Prayer: *In comparison to eternity, I am still as a young babe, Father. I love the life You have given me, and I am hopeful of the time when I will live in a glorified body, but with the wisdom You have bestowed still steadfastly residing inside. Amen.*

You Never Know What Might Come Up

The heart knows its own bitterness,
and a stranger does not share its joy.
Proverbs 14:10

When it comes to gardening, we try to be frugal, but it can get pricey whether we are watching our pennies or not. We repurpose and recycle and reuse everything we can, and that includes dirt. Some experts will tell you to throw out used dirt, since it may carry some disease or pests that will transfer to your new plantings. In some cases, we do send it to the compost pile, but unless our plants have shown some sign that we shouldn't, we reuse the dirt when transplanting.

Such was the case when we increased the size of our garden and added a small birdbath garden to our yard. We used what we had and then some. As the plants grew and matured, I noticed flowers growing in the garden that I had not planted. Among the marigolds that surrounded my veggie garden, I found both verbena and impatiens, and in the birdbath garden was a purple shamrock.

Roots and possibly seed from the dirt's previous tenants had sprouted and grown all on their own . . . well, sort of. Remember the seed principle I've mentioned before. This was a bonus, a happy surprise in my garden. However, it could just as easily have been weeds or grass that sprouted, and it would've been necessary to invest some time and work in pulling them out and keeping them from returning.

Sometimes we let things take root that we shouldn't. An offense, a hurt, or a rejection can become a root of bitterness deep on the inside, but guess what? It doesn't stay inside. It shows up on the outside too. It manifests in anger, depression, or just a generally nasty disposition.

Hurt people hurt people. Even good people who are hurt will hurt others. Don't let those bad seeds and roots take hold. Give them to Father, and take care of it now. Weed it out and throw it in the compost pile so that you don't hurt those around you or cut yourself off from people you can help, love, and enjoy. Sow only the good seeds down in your spirit. Let them take root, and then what shows up on the outside will be beautiful and wonderfully fragrant.

Prayer: *Father, please illuminate those offenses I harbor in my soul. I give them to You, and I thank You for opportunities to be a blessing to others. Amen.*

The Inheritance

The older women likewise, that they be reverent in behavior, not slanderers, not given to much wine, teachers of good things—that they admonish the young women to love their husbands, to love their children, to be discreet, chaste, homemakers, good, obedient to their own husbands, that the word of God may not be blasphemed.
Titus 2:3–5

I've always thought it was a good thing to learn from books, and I have done so. However, the ultimate mode of learning for me is to sit at the feet of an older, wiser woman, someone who has "been there, done that," and benefit from their years of experience.

As a small child, I literally did sit at the feet of my great-grandmother Adeline Johnson, aka "Mammy Johnson." I was enthralled by her. Born in 1889, she was a blast from the past. It was such a privilege to have a direct connection that far back in time, and through her I had access to firsthand knowledge of another way of life that otherwise would never have been available to me. I still hear her voice in my head sometimes, especially in the garden, and not a day goes by that I don't utilize something she taught me, think of her, or mention her to someone.

When I decided to get serious about gardening and opened myself up to learning about it more extensively, heavenly Father put in my path several ladies who not only had the knowledge, but also loved the garden in a way that imprinted on me. I think that, as much as the information itself, was what I was really looking for deep down inside.

Mrs. Betty Davis and Mike's great-aunt Mary Jane Page were both instrumental in my gardening instruction, and they both lovingly gave me their time (and perennial cuttings) to help me get started. They both displayed a reverential delight in passing this wisdom on to someone else who was interested and willing to be invested in gardening in the same way they had been.

Likewise, I have had great women of faith who invested time in me and taught me well the things of the Spirit and Scripture. Dr. Margaret Bomar planted a love of the Word in me and opened my eyes to the perfection of the Scriptures and the unequivocal assurance of salvation through faith in Jesus Christ. She did so lovingly and delightfully, and she never tired of answering my questions.

We may not be good gardeners or experts on Scripture, but God plants in each of us a gift of some kind, and He is very efficient in doing so. Utilizing our gifts brings us peace and keeps us sane. But passing them on, sharing them, that brings us joy. Sowing our gifts into the lives of others is what we were meant to do. It becomes an inheritance of sorts. You may think you don't have anything of value to offer a less experienced person, but I'm convinced you do. I know I do. As a token of appreciation of what has been given to me, I pass it on. I hope you will too.

Prayer: *Thank You, Lord, for all the wonderful gifts you have bestowed upon me and for the people you sent to deliver them. I am blessed beyond measure to pass them on. Amen.*

In the Fall of the Year

But of that day and hour no one knows, not even the angels in heaven,
nor the Son, but only the Father. Take heed, watch and pray;
for you do not know when the time is. . . .
And what I say to you, I say to all: Watch!
Mark 13:32–33, 37

It's subtle. There is a lack of humidity in the air; you can't call it "crisp" just yet, but there is a fresh feel to the atmosphere. The breezes are perky, and a rogue leaf or two can be seen whipping across the road. The chirping of the crickets in the morning is more pronounced; it seems they are heralding something new to come. The wildlife seems newly awakened from their hot summer slumber. Itches and sniffles are an indicator that ragweed is in its final bloom of the year. There is a sense of hush, stillness like before you become fully awake in the morning. The signs all point to autumn.

I always get excited and poetic when the seasons are about to change. It's not much different from the feeling we get on New Year's Eve: change is coming, and we are hopeful, optimistic. The head clears a little, routines get changed, and we're ready to take on the world again. I love that anticipatory feeling.

But once we get into the routine of the new season, the new thing we are doing . . . well, you know what happens. Doldrums. *Is this all there is?* For the most part, we just keep doing whatever we are doing, staying in the routine or sticking with the program because that's just life. It is made up of those little days where we do the same thing, day in and day out. We know what to expect and it's comfortable, but the seasonal changes and holidays give us something to look forward to while we are living everyday life.

There is something even better to look forward to: Jesus is coming! So many folks get all twisted up in the *when* and the signs to look for. However, if I've learned one thing it is this: nobody knows when. If someone prophetically announces the exact hour and date, then I am most assured that is when it is *not* going to happen. Jesus said that even He himself did not know the hour. What Father expects from us is to be hopefully anticipating His return, but living our lives and going about His business anyway.

We may very well be in the autumn of history. Maybe the end is near, but regardless, we need to live our lives as though Jesus may come back tomorrow or one hundred years from now. I believe what really matters is how we live our lives today. The next time you ask yourself, *Is this all there is?* be reminded that no, Jesus is coming, and that is all the excitement you need.

Prayer: *I don't need more time, Father. I just need You. Help me to be watchful and to live my life in a way that honors You, no matter when Jesus is to return. Amen.*

Transplanting 101

Enlarge the place of your tent, and let them stretch out the curtains of your dwellings; do not spare; lengthen your cords, and strengthen your stakes. For you shall expand to the right and to the left, and your descendants will inherit the nations.
Isaiah 54:2–3

When a plant has been in one spot or pot too long, it needs a little reviving. It needs a bigger, fresher place to establish itself. It gets root-bound, and the roots need to be able to stretch out and enable the plant to grow bigger. It needs a change. From the top, these plants can still look well established and healthy—full, leafy, maybe even flowering. They adapt and become accustomed to the stale underpinning and continue, amazingly, to flourish. But underneath, the soil has lost its nutritive value; it has hardened and dried and doesn't give the plant a healthy foundation.

Transplanting makes me a little nervous. It is precarious. All kinds of things—bad things—can happen. There are ways to transplant and minimize shock to the plant, and over the years I have learned a few tricks. Though I know what to do, I still feel a little uneasy because the outcome of a beautiful living thing is in my hands. No matter what level of care and expertise I employ, the outcome is still, like all gardening, unpredictable at best.

Sometimes, wonderfully, the plant will show little or no sign of shock after the transplant. Sometimes it will wilt for a few weeks and then bounce back. Sometimes leaves will die or turn yellow and will have to be pruned off. And then sometimes the unthinkable happens and the plant doesn't recover. Now I know that there are folks with much, much more gardening and plant-care expertise who would tell me that if any of the negative happens, it is my fault, that I've done something wrong to cause the demise of a seemingly healthy plant. And they are probably right. I'm still learning.

Life, and what we are doing with our lives, gets stale. We get into ruts and need to make a change. We may be flourishing and look like we've "got it going on," but deep down our roots are bound. We're not stretching and branching out; we're not challenging ourselves and exercising our faith. Father God is not glorified in a stagnated life. He expects us to be bold, to step out of our comfort zones, to embrace change, to meet challenges—and conquer them. He expects us to allow ourselves to be transplanted. When He is the gardener doing the transplanting, the shock will be minimal or nonexistent, and the outcome will be absolutely wonderful.

Prayer: *Father, You know I am averse to change. I get into my comfort zone and don't allow myself to be challenged or embrace something new. Help me to overcome my fears of the unknown, to be bold and to do greater things for You. Amen.*

A Pansy in the Snow

"Come now and let us reason together," says the LORD,
"though your sins are like scarlet, they shall be as white as snow."
Isaiah 1:18

When I was a rookie gardener, I made the decision to seek the counsel of someone very experienced in gardening, a fellow Mother's Day Out teacher, Mrs. Elise Reynolds. I asked so many questions, all of which she fielded with much patience and love.

At one point, I was particularly interested in fall plantings and had become fascinated with pansies, which are in such abundance every autumn (at least in middle Tennessee). I asked my mentor if she thought pansies would survive the winter, and she answered me, "I've seen pansies bloom in the snow."

A good student never forgets what the teacher has told her, and so I've always been confident in planting my pansies in the fall. We have an old iron pot that was my great-grandmother's, and over the years we've planted numerous varieties of annuals in it. One year in particular, I did a fall planting in it with an assortment of hardy winter plants, including beautiful royal-purple pansies.

In our part of the country, snow is not a regular event. However, that year we were privileged to see a side of nature that we rarely get to see and, except for the inconvenience of it, is a truly beautiful sight to behold. In the course of just a few hours, a swift and dramatic snowfall brought us a beautiful reminder of how God can make things fresh and new again.

When the snow clouds came, they dumped a good four inches right into my iron pot, and my plants disappeared for several days. By the third day, like a child coming up for air after hiding under a blanket for too long, there was a purple bloom, a stark and stunning contrast to the brilliant white of the receding snow. I was surprised it looked so healthy and vibrant, but then I remembered the words of my gardening mentor: "I've seen pansies bloom in the snow." Now that I had seen it for myself, not only was I reminded that my mentor knew what she was talking about (thanks, Mrs. Elise!), but I was reminded once again that God built into nature a language that teaches us about Him and ourselves and the relationship between the two.

Each of us is a work of art, simply because of the Artist who created us. Our true beauty doesn't show to its fullest until we allow the Father to blanket us in His goodness and perfection by the blood of Jesus and through the subsequent work of the Holy Spirit. He washes us white as snow, and His masterpiece then emerges, just like a brilliant purple pansy in the snow.

Prayer: *You have washed me white as snow, Lord, and I thank You. I pray that Your beauty and majesty, even if it is just a glimpse, will shine through my life each and every day. Amen.*

The Perennial Gardener

*The LORD will guide you continually, and satisfy your soul in drought,
and strengthen your bones; you shall be like a watered garden,
and like a spring of water, whose waters do not fail.*
Isaiah 58:11

As a greenhorn, I practiced my gardening technique on various annuals such as impatiens, petunias, geraniums, and salvias—and don't forget my favorite, morning glories. Of course, I still do enjoy all these beauties every year. Their variety of color and texture gives depth and personality to my gardens. However, as my knowledge increased and expertise progressed, I learned a little gardener's secret: perennials. These are the plants and flowers that come back every year. You don't have to go to the nursery to buy a new crop every spring, just to watch them die off in the fall, never to be admired again.

There is more to a perennial plant than meets the eye. I would say that these plants have virtues, if you will allow me in a poetic sense to personify them a bit. Perennials are faithful to come back every year. Perennials replicate themselves; you put one plant in, and in a few years you have a garden full. Perennials are resilient; they stand up to drought, and many of them survive the hottest sun or deepest shade, depending upon their variety. Better than most, they fight off the pests and diseases that attack the garden. Their blooms can be short-lived and their vibrancy fleeting; however, there is a different, long-lasting beauty in the color, texture, and shape of their leaves, which enhances the garden for most of the year.

Likewise, we can share in these virtues of the perennial. We can be faithful to God in service and function, replicating ourselves through our Christian witness and by introducing others to Jesus. We should be resilient in order to withstand the tribulations of life, and as we establish and age, our appearance transforms from the vivid brilliancy of youth to one of texture, depth, and steadfastness.

These virtues don't come from the ground, the sun, the rain, or, most especially, ourselves. They come from the Gardener Himself. He is faithful, and He never lets us down (Deuteronomy 7:9). He reproduces Himself in us; as we mature, we become more like Him (Ephesians 2:10). He never changes; no matter the time or the climate, He is always the same

(Malachi 3:6). He is not swayed or deterred by His enemies, for He is their Creator as well (Isaiah 54:16–17). God is forever beautiful, mighty, and unwavering. He is a wonderful, gentle, and loving gardener, and He takes great delight in tending and watching over us, His perennial garden.

Prayer: *Father, I bless You for your patience and care in teaching me about You, life, myself, and Your garden. I praise You for Your faithfulness, tenderness, and loving-kindness, and I thank You for always being there, ready to strengthen, guide, and love us all. Amen.*

Watching Over the Household

Proverbs 31:27

The Family Tree

O LORD, You are the portion of my inheritance and my cup. . . .
Yes, I have a good inheritance.
Psalm 16:5–6

If your family is anything like mine, you probably have someone in the family who has done a genealogy search of some kind. We have been very fortunate on both sides of our family to have had very diligent folk who have worked long and hard to come up with lots of interesting information about our heritage.

For instance, we have discovered that our daughter, Sally, is eligible for the Daughters of the American Revolution (DAR) through not one, but two branches of the family tree. We are proud that she has two ancestors, Lemuel Perrin and Christian Waldschmidt, who were Patriot fighters in the Revolutionary War.

Our son, William Murphy Grenley, is particularly proud that he is named after his great- grandfather John Murphy Dean, who was named after his great-uncle Judge John Murphy of Akron, Ohio. The judge was a Civil War hero; he carried the colors for the North at Antietam and was wounded in the effort. He is one of the few heroes of the Civil War who received a Congressional Medal of Honor. Will is now the proud owner of that medal.

There is a story on every branch of the family tree—some good, some not so good. We have our share of stories of bootleggers and horse thieves, as well. We even have an ongoing family joke that my husband Mike and I are related, and in fact, we are; we share the same fifth great- grandfather, Allen Neal. We did not discover this interesting (and maybe unfortunate) fact until we had been married for ten years. So, I am married to my distant cousin. You may now make all the jokes you like about me being from the South.

Every family has a history, even if it hasn't yet been discovered. We all have a heritage, an ancestry; we all came from somewhere. When you open the Bible to read Matthew's account of the birth of Christ, you find a genealogy, which is a record of the ancestors of Jesus. When the Holy Spirit inspired this writing, God saw fit to make a historical record of those important names, for many reasons, I'm sure—one being to reveal that

Jesus' human ancestry was the fulfillment of prophecy, proving that He was who He said He was.

When we become Christians, we are reborn into a new, adopted family, one that is beyond our earthly ancestry. We have a new heritage; God is our Father, and we become joint heirs with Jesus Christ. It is very important to be mindful of this fact: not only are we new creations, but we are in a new family as well, a royal one. We may not know the account of our earthly ancestry; circumstances may prevent us from finding out. But thanks to the Word of God, we can know the origin of our heavenly family and that we now have a heritage that is pure, stable, and eternal.

Prayer: *Lord, You are Father to me. I want to thank You for giving me a heavenly family and the assurance that one day I will be with them all. Amen.*

New Beginnings

If we confess our sins, He is faithful and just to forgive us our sins and to cleanse us from all unrighteousness.
1 John 1:9

I admit it—I am not a high-tech gal. Ask anyone I've worked with and they will confirm this truth about me. But even so, I decided a long time ago that my computer is a wonderful thing. I can correspond with friends, run a business, write a newsletter . . . or a book, send an electronic greeting card, and best of all, I can play games!

Early on, I discovered a game on my computer that became my absolute favorite. It's called Free Cell. Many of you are probably familiar with it; it's a type of Solitaire, great fun and a wonderful way to clear the mind and relieve a little stress. One of the best features of this game is a thing called "restart." If you get stuck and can't make any more moves as a result of some bad decisions you made early on in the hand, you can return to the beginning of the same hand and start again. You can remember where you took the wrong turn, avoid those same mistakes, and usually win on the second or third (or many times, for me) try. I love that—I'm always a winner.

Because we are human, we often make wrong moves. Let's face it—we mess up, we fail, we sin. What I have come to realize is that God is more interested in our getting up than our falling down. He wants us to be victorious. True, He wants nothing to do with sin, but because He sent Jesus, He forgives us and gives us a restart when we fail. Even if we make the same dumb mistake again, He is quick to forgive and cleanse us the minute we ask Him. Quicker than the "click of a mouse" (that's me speaking "techie"), the restart is in place. We can start fresh and, hopefully, be a little wiser and not make all the wrong moves again.

When my children were growing up, I would tell them, "Today is a new day. We have a clean slate. Everything that happened yesterday is gone." That's what God does every time we fail Him. He gives us a clean slate, a restart. The Bible says, "We are more than conquerors through Him who loved us" (Romans 8:37). That means, because of Jesus, we're winners, and we have the victory all the time.

Prayer: *Father, please forgive me where I have failed You. I thank You for the many, many second chances You have given me in my life, and I thank You that in You I have the victory. Amen.*

Me First!

But many who are first will be last, and the last first.
Matthew 19:30

It's funny how our language evolves as our children get older. There are so many words and phrases that I no longer say that were once used to direct them when they were small: "use your inside voice"; "we hold hands in the parking lot"; and "don't be a me-first Milly!" I was reminded of this last phrase while I was shopping during the holidays.

I was third or fourth in the checkout line, patiently waiting for my turn to pay, when a man walked up, his arms loaded with his purchases. He stood slightly ahead of me and to my left. When the person who was at the head of the line moved up, the man simply maneuvered to his right and broke line in front of me.

Now I have to be honest. My very first inclination was to say, "Hey, bub! The back of the line is that way!" But something tugged at my heart a bit, and I decided to evaluate the situation before taking action. It occurred to me that this man might not be from this country; maybe his traditions and customs didn't include waiting your turn. Or maybe his family's social graces went by a different set of rules; maybe he had ten siblings and it was "every man for himself" in his family of origin. Maybe they didn't teach manners and politeness where he went to kindergarten, if he had even had the opportunity to go to kindergarten.

I admit I was feeling a little huffy, a bit impatient, and rather irritated. But then that still, small voice in my heart said, "What's your hurry?" I realized once again that God is watching and using even the smallest circumstance as a mirror before us so that we can see we haven't come all that far after all. It was just like back in grammar school when I was standing in line and wanting to tell the teacher the little boy had cut in front of me. I felt a little grin begin to rise up from my heart and out to my mouth. I had to take a moment to laugh at myself a little and then be gracious to someone who may or may not have knowingly just taken advantage of me.

God expects us to grow up and learn to take the high road and turn the other cheek. That process of being "perfected," as the Bible puts it, happens as we are tested time and time again in the little things. Learning patience, giving, graciousness, and sacrifice is part of growing in the Lord. Look for those little tests and be glad; they are opportunities to grow and to know that God is watching and cheering you on.

Prayer: *It is a blessing, Father, to give You first place in my life. I don't mind standing at the back of the line for You. Amen.*

The Can-Do Attitude

I can do all things through Christ who strengthens me.
Philippians 4:13

For her birthday one year, our daughter, Sally, wanted to take a group of friends ice-skating. Our son Will is almost five years younger than his sister and was accustomed to (and willing to be) the tagalong to any and all girl-type activities. Amazingly, he still doesn't mind tagging along with his big sister.

I have never ice-skated and had no intention of joining the group on the ice. I was observing from the safety of the stands overlooking the rink. Mike was experienced at ice-skating and was delegated the task of taking Will, who was about four years old, onto the ice for his first ice-skating lesson.

The girls were already skating amid the horde of Saturday-afternoon birthday-party skaters, and Mike had gotten Will's skates properly fitted onto his little feet and turned his attention to putting on his own skates. He was looking down and focused on the task at hand when, to my horror, I saw Will take off across the ice and into the path of all the skaters as he made his way to the center of the rink.

It was noisy. Mike could not hear me yelling to get his attention. When he completed his task, he looked up and, realizing Will was nowhere to be found, looked up at me to see if I had been watching. I was working my way down toward the ice, yelling and pointing to where Will was. His eyes followed the direction of my pointing, and his eyes almost bugged out of his head at the sight. In the course of my panic and Mike's busy oblivion, Will had watched the other skaters who were practicing skating backwards in the center of the ice and then started to do likewise. It appeared that Will didn't need any lessons after all.

In his innocence, Will assumed he could do what everyone else was doing—and he did. Not once did it occur to him that he might not be able to ice-skate, forwards or backwards. He did it and he did it well, especially for a four-year-old on ice skates for the first time. Needless to say, Mike quickly scurried across the ice to retrieve our little boy out of harm's way.

140

We all need that kind of determined confidence. We face challenges; we must try new things, take on new tasks, face the unknown, and move forward. We can't let fear or lack of ability stop us when God's got our backs. There is a saying I love: "God doesn't call people who can. He calls people who will." He provides us with everything we need to get the job done. It's God who can do, and because He can, we just need to put on our skates and go along for the glide.

Prayer: *Lord, You are not an unknown to me. I know that I can count on You to get me through those new tasks and challenges, and if I fall, You are there to pick me up and help me move on. Amen.*

Scars into Beauty Marks

He has made everything beautiful in its time.
Ecclesiastes 3:11

I remember few details about my childhood, but the big stuff sticks in my mind and the unusual things as well. My maternal grandfather had a very unique physical feature, and I have not forgotten it. Poppy was a milkman (for you youngsters, that's someone who delivers milk to your front porch), and before I was born, he slammed the door of his milk truck on his thumb and it was amputated.

As sickening and morose as this sounds, rest assured, his thumb healed quite nicely and was not something that was terribly noticeable. There was a scar across the front of his nub where the skin had healed from the doctor's closing and stitching of his wound. This happened before I was born, so the state of Poppy's thumb was normal to me, part of who he was, and was not frightening to me at all. Sometimes I would sit in his lap and rub his scar lightly, carefully. He always loved that; I'm sure it was endearing to him that I was not repelled by his ugly nub but instead just accepted it and him as he was.

I had the privilege of hearing Anne Graham Lotz speak at a women's conference once. Something she said still sticks in my mind today. She said that in heaven our scars will be turned into beauty marks, and I believe that with all my heart. But there is one set of scars that I believe will remain as they are—the scars on Jesus' hands, feet, and side. I don't believe they will change. They will remain as a reminder to us of what He has done for us.

In Jesus' day, the cross was a place of shame and ugliness. What we see from our vantage point is that it was a place of grace and mercy designed for our salvation. Even though Jesus' scars will not have changed in appearance when we see them for the first time, they will be as beauty marks to us—symbols of His grace, mercy, and love that abound toward us in immeasurable amounts.

My hope is that someday Jesus will allow me to kiss those hands, lightly and lovingly touch His scars, and look at what the world would consider ugly, but to me are wondrous beauty marks that made the way for me to know Him personally and forever.

Prayer: *Father, I can never know the full extent of the pain and suffering that Jesus experienced on my behalf. I am thankful beyond measure for Your love and sacrifice. Amen.*

Sinking Sand

Jesus Christ is the same yesterday, today, and forever.
Hebrews 13:8

We live in troubling times. Evil appears to be escalating. Civil unrest has increased exponentially in recent years; people are being sold into slavery; religious radicals are brutally slaughtering their enemies in record numbers; wicked regimes are taking over governments and causing worldwide chaos; and poverty, famine, natural disasters, and disease continue to increase. It is difficult to watch a regular newscast and not become depressed and fearful.

It is also true that the standards in our country have significantly changed. Our family values and principles have deteriorated ominously over the last fifty years, and the increased crime and divorce rates, as well as our indifference to today's morals, are symptomatic of these changes. I know that if I was young again and considering having a child, I would have to do some serious soul-searching before deciding to bring a baby into this dark and sinister world. If you have small children or grandchildren, you may be wondering with much trepidation what the world will be like when they grow up.

If you will search the Scriptures, you might notice something interesting. In Jesus' day, the times and state of the world were not so different from today. Evil dictators ruled, people were enslaved and mistreated, and genocide was the norm. Brutality, poverty, famine, and disease—all were prevalent in Bible times. The state of affairs was very similar to what we are experiencing now, and it appears we are devolving to the malevolence of that prior age.

How do we maintain our peace in the midst of all this turbulence and disorder? How do we even keep our sanity? There is only one answer: inner peace comes from knowing that while everything else is unstable, our God never changes. The same God who created the universe, the same God who parted the Red Sea, the same God who became a man by the name of Jesus and died on a cross for our sins and rose again is the same God who rules and reigns today. He is the same God for all times—past, present, and future. He does not change. We can rest assured in that truth. He still works miracles, still heals broken bodies and broken hearts, still restores relationships, and still loves, provides, and cares for His people. He. Does. Not. Change.

One of my favorite hymns reminds us that no matter what is going on around us, we can depend on God to stay the same. The chorus goes like this:

> On Christ the solid Rock, I stand
> All other ground is sinking sand,
> All other ground is sinking sand.

I'm standing on the rock of my salvation. No matter what else happens in this world, I can rely on Him to never change, and you can too.

Prayer: *Father I believe You never change, and that is my greatest comfort. Amen.*

The Right of Way

*Because narrow is the gate and difficult is the way
which leads to life, and there are few who find it.*
Matthew 7:14

Back in my carpool days, when school let out every afternoon, the traffic in the little town where we lived would come to a standstill. What was normally a ten-minute drive would easily increase to a thirty-minute commute. There was a side street, however, that would cut down that jammed-up drive home by almost ten minutes. The only drawback in taking the shortcut was that in order to get back onto the main thoroughfare from the side street, you had to make a left turn into bumper-to-bumper traffic without the benefit of a traffic light.

There was one little catch to making that turn back into traffic: I had to believe, before I committed myself to go the back way, that there would be someone nice enough to wave me on and would sit still to let me go ahead. I admit that I always got a little nervous as I approached the intersection. I always held my breath as I waited for the kind soul who had taken the long way around instead of the shortcut to stop and let me in.

Fortunately for me, and speaking well of the folks in that town, there was always someone who would indeed let me slide in ahead of them, and they often let several other short-cutters in at the same time. I would give them a friendly "thank you" wave, and very often they would wave back their "you're welcome." After that, the ride home was not so long and wearisome, thanks to someone who demonstrated a little grace to an impatient, but thankful short-cutter.

One day as I was waiting for my daily dose of traffic grace, I realized this was a picture of what God did for us. When Jesus came to earth, He lived perfectly and died for our sins, something we are unable to do on our own. He took the long way around for us. When it comes time for us to be heading "home," He will stop "traffic" and give us the right of way, even though we don't deserve it. In order to access this heavenly shortcut, we have to believe that He took the long way around for us, that He is a man of His word and will let us go home, free and clear.

I am still very grateful for the shortcut home from school, for the Good Samaritans who were kind enough to let me back into traffic, and for the almighty King of all creation who took the long, hard way for me and became my right of way to heaven. No doubt, when I arrive, there will be a very friendly wave—a "thank you" from me, and I know He'll wave back at me with a wonderfully sweet and gracious "you're welcome."

Prayer: *Father, life has very few shortcuts, and the road home is a long one. I thank You for making the way for me to get there safe and sound. Amen.*

The Job's Not Done Until Daddy Bleeds

*But now in Christ Jesus you who once were far off have been
brought near by the blood of Christ.*
Ephesians 2:13

My husband, Mike, is like a bull in a china shop. He is very physical, works hard, and takes charge and jumps in with both feet before thinking it through. He's a gung-ho, all-hands-on-deck, man-the-torpedoes, manly kind of man. If it needs doing, he's your guy. Now, he is *not* Mr. Fix It. He is competent, but not necessarily gifted in mechanical things. He will get the job done . . . eventually.

When our kids were little, Mike was the first one out of bed and up the stairs if one of the children was having a nightmare. Without a second thought, he'd be in the car and at the drugstore picking up the prescription the doctor called in during the night. If a damsel is in distress (usually me), he stops immediately and helps out. If someone, anyone, is stranded on the road, he stops and makes sure they have help coming. Our children nicknamed him "Mr. Happy Coffee" because of his energy and over-the-top enthusiasm.

Over the years, the kids—and I admit, I, too—have had a good laugh at his expense when his gusto went awry and the incident at hand took a slapstick turn. He has been known to drop a log on his thumb, break his toe falling down the stairs, and set himself ablaze lighting a brush fire— and nearly blowing up the neighborhood in the process. And countless— yes, countless—times he has cut or in some other minor way maimed himself in finishing a project. Thus one of our family mantras has become and forever will be "the job is not done till Daddy bleeds."

Jesus had a mission. There was a plan and a purpose for His time here on earth. He made His mission clear to us in Luke 4:18-19:

The Spirit of the LORD is upon Me,
Because He has anointed Me
To preach the gospel to the poor;
He has sent Me to heal the brokenhearted,
To proclaim liberty to the captives
And recovery of sight to the blind,
To set at liberty those who are oppressed;

To proclaim the acceptable year of the Lord.

It took energy, resolve, and a servant's heart to get the job done. Jesus had it. He was a manly man, and without hesitation, He jumped right in and completed the task. In order to finish the job, He had to bleed. He poured out every drop of His blood for us. It was no laughing matter; our salvation was at His expense, and wonderfully, thankfully, He chose it.

Prayer: *You chose us all, Father. You bled for us all, Jesus. You comfort and guide us by Your Spirit, Lord. Thank You for everything. Amen.*

A Gift of Love

I will instruct you and teach you in the way you should go;
I will guide you with My eye. Psalm 32:8

If you parent, you teach. Teaching is not just instruction of a skill. It is guiding, nurturing, and protecting. It is promotion of independence. Teaching never stops. Even now, though our children are grown and away from us, I find that we are still teaching them. They learn from our experience, and they also learn not to make the mistakes we made by observing us suffering the consequences. They ask questions, and it is an honor to be able to answer them.

The best part of teaching is that you also learn as you teach. When the children were little, I could look into their eyes and see what God intended for me to be: pure of heart, completely trusting and adoring of those who cared to nurture them. They had a perfect and pure love and were so open to God. As they grew and became more independent, I learned to trust God more—to see my children as human and fallible, and to come to terms with them understanding the same about me. I had to learn to take my hands off and to let go and let God.

The disciples called Jesus "Teacher." His time on earth was limited, so every moment was a teaching opportunity. He spent His time wisely and left stories, prayers, and experiences behind to continue the teaching process through the ages. We open our Bibles, and He is still teaching us, guiding us, protecting us. He knows we are fallible. We can count on Him to be infallible and to always be our teacher.

If it hadn't been for teaching, I wouldn't have known the wonder of a butterfly, the miracle of a bubble, the beauty of a lullaby, or the excitement of watching a seed grow. If it weren't for teaching, I wouldn't know the blessing of drying a tear, the *a-ha* moments of realization, the lingering bittersweet feeling of a good-bye hug.

If it hadn't been for learning, my life would be unfulfilled, empty, and colorless. If it hadn't been for learning, I wouldn't know my Savior, my assurance of everlasting life, and the safety and security of being a child of God. I'm grateful that God made me a teacher; it is truly one of His greatest gifts. I'm grateful that He is my teacher and that He is the greatest gift of all.

Prayer: *Thank You, Lord, for every teachable moment in my life. I have learned from them all. Amen.*

Distorted Reality

For our light affliction, which is but for a moment, is working for us a far more exceeding and eternal weight of glory, while we do not look at the things which are seen, but at the things which are not seen. For the things which are seen are temporary, but the things which are not seen are eternal.
2 Corinthians 4:17–18

You can tell a lot about a person by the way they drive, what they drive, and the condition of the car they are driving. You can even tell a person's faith and politics by the bumper stickers on their car. No, I'm not talking about judging others by the condition of their vehicles. You never know where others are in life, but I think a lot of times their vehicles are extensions of themselves.

For instance, if I see someone in a bright-red sports car, I'm thinking they are bold rather than shy; maybe they like adventure. If I see a dirty, unkempt, maybe dinged-up type of vehicle, then aesthetics probably aren't important to them, or maybe they have more vital things on their agenda. Everyone is different, but I think very often you can tell what is happening on the inside by what you see on the outside.

I was sitting at a stoplight in heavy traffic one day, minding my own business, probably singing along to a song on the radio. I noticed that my mirrors and windows seemed to be pulsating as a result of the loud bass of a nearby car stereo, and in my peripheral vision, I could see a large white truck steering slowly into the middle of the road between the lanes. As I glanced back, I noticed a teenage boy driving the oversized, detailed, and I'm sure very expensive truck. He was obviously taunting someone behind me and threatening to cut them off.

I quickly moved my car up and out of harm's way and said a quick prayer for this not to turn into a "situation." After the light changed and we moved forward, I could clearly see his back window with the detailed lettering: DISTORTED REALITY. I'm not very hip about these things. For all I know, this could be the name of some kind of music group or marketing ploy. But I thought to myself, *Now, there you go. What an appropriate phrase and how fitting for the back window of a road bully.*

We live in a different world these days. Our reality, especially after 9-11, has changed. This new perspective can convince us that we are subject to bullies and to threats of violence and acts of terrorism, and creates in us a victim mentality. There is not a region of our country that hasn't been affected in some way by these acts. Whether the experience has taken place in a movie theater, a college campus, or even a grammar school, the threat is a reality everywhere.

How can we go on without fear? Truly, we must be wise, take precautions, and not be foolish in this natural and evil world. But the Bible tells us that the seen is temporary, while the unseen is eternal. The spiritual reality is that there is a war going on that we do not see. There are ministering spirits, angels, all about us, and they engage in battles daily on our behalf.

Father doesn't promise us that our lives will be trouble free; in fact, Jesus assured us that we would indeed experience tribulation. Nonetheless, God is watching over us, and nothing is going to happen to us that He does not permit. We must be mindful of this and not allow what is seen with our eyes to make us victims to the bullies of this world, both great and small. The truth is, God loves us, and in Him we have a different reality where we can feel safe.

Enjoy your life. Be anxious for nothing. And don't forget to wash your car.

Prayer: *You, Lord, are the Almighty. Father, I ask Your Holy Spirit to minister to those who are victims of evil and bullies. May You be the Lord of them and their aggressors. In You we have all the safety and security we need. Amen.*

Whatever You Need, God Is

And my God shall supply all your need according to
His riches in glory by Christ Jesus.
Philippians 4:19

I take pride in being an organized person, although you can't always tell it by the way my house looks, especially my plastic-ware cabinet. My husband is definitely the zealous organizer in the family, and hopefully that has rubbed off on me a little over the years.

Around our house, we have a few little systems in place that, if used correctly, help to run the household in a more efficient way. One of those systems is the use of a dry- erase board on our refrigerator. When we run out of an item, the routine is to write it on the dry-erase board, and then when the time comes to make our shopping list, the things we need are already listed there for us. That way we don't forget anything when we are at the store.

Now, it works really well if I follow the plan, but sadly, I can't tell you the number of times I have called from the store to ask what was written on the board. It is such a simple thing, and when implemented, it takes the pressure off having to remember what the family needs. For certain, *something* is always written on that board.

I was walking through the kitchen one day and glanced at the refrigerator, noticing something very peculiar. For once, the dry-erase board was completely devoid of any black scribbles. I thought to myself, *That's strange—we don't need anything!* If I had taken an inventory of the cupboards and refrigerator at that moment, I'm sure we would have indeed needed something, but it wasn't apparent from the condition of the board.

There's a song I love called "Whatever You Need, God Is." God doesn't just take care of and fulfill our needs; He Himself replaces them. Often, when we think we need some *thing*, we really only need *Him*. I have countless testimonies of the faithfulness of God and how He has met my needs over the years. Whether it was something as tangible as a paycheck or as intangible as a hug, He has always made a way to reach out of the supernatural and into the natural to take care of that very thing I've needed. Even still, with all the proof of His reliability, I still find myself worrying about whether He will meet my latest need or help me answer the latest challenge.

I look forward to the day when the dry-erase board of my heart remains clean except for the word *God*. All my confidence will be in the fact that as long as I have Him, I have no need. The Bible says that He knows what our needs are (Matthew 6:8). He doesn't need a little white dry-erase board to help Him remember, and He certainly doesn't need a list. He requires only our faith in Him to get the job done.

Whatever need you have today, God is the answer to it. You can certainly be thankful that you have a loving Creator who loves you and will meet all your needs.

Prayer: *My greatest need, Father, is to know You and to experience Your presence. Beyond that, I require nothing else for my sustenance, happiness, or contentment. You have already taken care of it all. Amen.*

His Banner over Me Is Love

He brought me to the banqueting house,
and his banner over me was love.
Song of Solomon 2:4

A few years ago, there were news reports of a Nashville businessman, a car dealer, who had been called on the carpet by city officials for flying too many American flags on the antennae of the automobiles in his lot and for displaying (as considered by the law) a distracting number of banners at his place of business. Fortunately, this very patriotic entrepreneur stood strong for his beliefs and maintained his position in a very public and courageous way, resulting in the city seeing fit to allow him to continue to express his patriotism as he wished.

It seems these days, banners are being flown everywhere. American flags are seen on the lapels of coats and jackets and on blue jeans, hair ribbons, book bags, cars, houses, signs in yards, and even on doggie sweaters. Until recent years, I don't recall a time when the American symbol of courage and freedom has been flown and displayed in such a proud way by such a large number of citizens.

This flag, this banner, reminds us of those who have died for the freedoms we enjoy and is a declaration that we will not be afraid of what the future may hold, for we are "one nation, under God, indivisible." Whenever a banner is flown in such a manner, it stands for something—something important, something victorious, something eternal. Therefore, the flag has become our identification with freedom, bravery, and personal sacrifice.

Another word for banner is *standard*. A standard can be a flag, but it is also a measure, something against which we gauge ourselves. As Christians, we look to God as our standard; it is His character that is our measuring stick, our benchmark. The word *Christian*, after all, means "little Christ." One of God's covenant names is Jehovah Nissi, "the Lord is my banner." He reveals Himself to us as our standard and our victor. He is our measure, and under Him and in Him, we are victorious.

Also, the Bible says, "God is love" (1 John 4:16). If God is our standard and He is love, then our standard must also be love. We must live in and operate by the love that He has shown us by His sacrifice of Jesus on the cross, and by how He blesses us, forgives us, and keeps all His promises to us. That love holds for us a place of protection and gives us the victory we need in our lives to keep moving forward as standard-bearers, soldiers carrying His banner. As faithful followers, we should display this banner proudly, with just as much fervor, dedication, and boldness as that with which we fly Old Glory.

From now on, I think an American flag, among other things, will be my personal symbol of God's love. It will be a reminder to me to walk more in His love and to share it more with others, and to courageously and publicly stand strong for my beliefs, demonstrating God's love as I march forward under His banner every day.

Prayer: *Help me to demonstrate Your love to others, Father, to reveal who You are to the part of the world I am able to touch. Amen.*

The Finishing Touch

I thank God upon every remembrance of you . . .
being confident of this very thing, that He who has begun
a good work in you will complete it until the day of Jesus Christ.
Philippians 1:3, 6

Mike and I are not "with it" hipster types. Our idea of the nightlife is sitting around a campfire. It won't surprise you, then, to find out that we like to watch those home-and- garden shows on television. We used to enjoy one in particular that introduced artisans of all types who were extremely gifted and skilled in unique crafts of different sorts. One particular episode stood out to me because of something one of the artists said about his work.

He was a sculptor who worked with iron and steel and made beautiful metal gates and statuary. Given the medium he used, his work was exquisitely delicate. He said that the difference between a good artist and a great one was in the details, and usually the very detailed work that made the difference was the last 10 percent of his work on any particular piece. In many cases, he could consider his work done when it was actually only about 90 percent completed, but it was the last 10 percent that made the work a true piece of art. He also found that this stage of the work was usually the most meticulous and precise work he would do on a piece.

We could apply this philosophy to any area of our lives, whether it is at our jobs, in our personal growth, in parenting or other relationships, or, most importantly, in our spiritual lives. If it is almost quitting time on a workday, if we are nearing retirement, if we are growing older, if we are raising almost-grown kids, if we've been married "forever," or if we've been Christians since we were children, there is an opportunity to get lazy and quit before the appointed time.

We are human. We have bodies and minds that get tired and weary. We may even get bored before we get to the end of a task or project. It is a mark of maturity to follow through, persevere, and stick with what we are doing and see it to its proper completion. We have the opportunity in everything we undertake to take part in creating a masterpiece, whether in our work, ourselves, or our children, if we will just stick with it and take care of that last 10 percent. It will set us apart from the rest.

Aren't you glad that God is a completer? I know I am. You find Him in the details, because He never leaves the last 10 percent of anything undone. The last words that Jesus spoke from the cross were "It is finished" (John 19:30). We have the assurance from the cross that God completes His work. We should follow His example in everything we endeavor to do; after all, God works on us until we are completely finished too.

Prayer: *Lord, please help me to finish everything I start and to not give up when I am getting close to the end. May my last 10 percent always be my best. Amen.*

Olly, Olly, Oxen Free

For nothing is secret that will not be revealed, nor anything hidden that will not be known and come to light.
Luke 8:17

Olly, olly, oxen free! Do you remember that phrase? It's what you yelled when you were "it" in a game of hide-and-seek and you called in all the "hiders" to return, free and clear.

As I've gotten older, I've come to realize more and more that many of the events in our lives, both big and small, are merely a series of "losts and founds." It really is like a big game of hide-and-seek. I just wonder how many hours I have spent looking for misplaced glasses, keys, important papers, jewelry, and old pictures. Then there is the bigger stuff: my mate, my children when they wander off, my car in parking lots, myself on unfamiliar roads, my dogs. You've been there, and you know the list can go on and on.

But there are those who are lost on an even greater and much more serious scale: kidnapped or missing children or adults, older folks with Alzheimer's who don't remember who or where they are and have wandered off, soldiers missing in action, and the souls of those who do not know Jesus. How sad it is that you can know where you are on the outside, but on the inside you can still be wandering aimlessly, looking for the way home.

We know we are lost if we don't have directions, a map, a guide, or a standard to follow. If we do not have someone from whom we can follow good directions, we get lost or just keep going in circles.

Our God is a God of the lost—lost things and, more importantly, lost people. We couldn't hide from Him if we tried. He sees us where we are, and He wants us where we are supposed to be. He is the direction, the guide, the standard, the way home. We might be spending what seems like an eternity looking for our keys, but we can know where we are and where we are going in Him. It's as though He is yelling, "Olly, olly, oxen free!" and beckoning us to come to Him. He brings us into the light where we are free and clear, and He keeps us there. We're no longer lost, and it's the safest, warmest place to be.

Prayer: *Father, thankfully, I am no longer lost. I have found my rightful place in Your loving and protective care, and that is where I want to be. I pray for all the lost people and things of the world. I know it is Your will that they be found. Amen.*

May I Have Your Attention, Please?

Be still, and know that I am God.
Psalm 46:10

A springtime chore that cannot be ignored is cleaning out the gutters along the roofline, and one warm spring morning, Mike decided it was time. I was working in the kitchen, and I could hear a lot of stomping around up above. The water was swishing through the gutters, and all of the debris was flying around. It was busy and sounded very "Mike like."

At some point, I could hear my husband's muffled voice. Considering that he is a very gregarious fellow and will talk to just about anybody, I assumed he was having a conversation with a neighbor or curious passerby, so I just continued about my business without giving it much thought.

For quite some time, I kept hearing his muffled voice, and the thought occurred to me that he was having quite the conversation with someone from up on that roof. After about five minutes, I really tuned my ears to the sound of his voice and noticed there was a curious cadence or rhythm to what he was saying, as though he was repeating the same words over and over. I was curious, intrigued, so I went out on the front walk to see what was going on.

And there he was. He had his hands cupped over his mouth, and he was yelling into one of the vent pipes that come out of the roof. He was yelling repeatedly, and by now frantically, "Help me! Help me!" Now, he wasn't acting out his version of the old movie *The Fly;* he really needed help! While he had been busily and, in typical Mike fashion, enthusiastically cleaning out the gutters, his ladder had slipped and fallen to the ground. He had no way of getting off the roof. The poor thing was stranded.

Just a side note here: The funniest part of this story is that our daughter left the house during this time, got into her car, and drove off. When he heard her start her car, thinking his rescue was imminent, he leaned over the edge of the roof closest to her car, waving his arms and hat to get her attention. Focused on leaving and getting to her destination, she didn't notice and sped away. Between her inattention and my ignoring his voice, he began to wonder if he might just have to spend the night up on that roof.

But I digress. Finally, after what had become quite the ordeal, I rescued my knight in shining armor . . . well, actually, knight in sweaty work clothes. All's well that ends well—except, of course, for the somewhat traumatized and aggravated husband.

I believe there are many times when God wants to get our attention, and we either hear and ignore Him or just stay so focused on going about our business that we don't make time to listen and be attentive. He desires our fellowship. He wants us to want to spend time with Him; He wants to bless us with His presence in our lives. He doesn't want us to involve Him only when there is an emergency or tragedy; He wants to be active and involved with us all the time.

Here is what I have come to understand about God's character: He doesn't force His way into our lives. We have to invite Him in and establish the connection ourselves. He made the way for that to happen by sending us Jesus; the rest is up to us. We can make a connection with God every day just by getting quiet and sitting still and listening. I assure you, He's calling. All we have to do is listen and answer.

Prayer: *Father, teach me to be attuned to Your voice. I know You have loving and wise words to say to me, and I don't want to miss a thing. Amen.*

Slower Traffic, Stay in the Right Lane

The plans of the diligent lead surely to plenty, but those of everyone who is hasty, surely to poverty.
Proverbs 21:5

After twenty long years of raising children, I found myself in the traditional workforce once again. I had to become accustomed to what I had successfully avoided for quite some time: rush-hour traffic. Now, when you are not comfortable with this cruel dynamic of the work world, it can be a great test of character as well as a shock to your system. Since the time of my last rush-hour commute, my town had grown significantly, and of course, so had the traffic. It took some concentrated adapting on my part.

There was an odd characteristic to the particular route I took each morning. It was directed toward a major intersection, which, with a left turn, took you toward the interstate. As a result, I found that the left lane, for quite a stretch of the road, was extremely congested with drivers who evidently were thinking ahead and getting into the left lane early. One of the rules of the road, according to my upbringing, was the slower traffic was to stay to the right, but every morning in this area of town, it was not the case. The slower traffic was always in the left lane.

Being new to the traffic world once again, and being the impatient sort that I am, it became my habit to drive in the right lane. Then, as I approached my left turn, I would find a window of opportunity to jump into the left lane. I was able to move along at a much steadier, smoother pace without a lot of starts and stops. In my mind, I felt like I was not stuck in traffic and stressed by that unfortunate reality.

Everyone knows that passing on the right lane, which is what I was essentially doing for miles, is dangerous. Besides, I wonder what I missed by zipping down the faster side of traffic, hoping to move left in time to make my turn. Maybe it was some valuable prayer time or a lesson from Father that was right before my eyes, or maybe it was a chance to set a good example or help someone.

"Slow but steady wins the race" is what the tortoise said to the hare. Rushing to get anywhere can lead us to blunder or disaster, whether we are driving or not. We live in a convenience-packed, drive-through world where you would think our time would be expanded. But it seems that all this convenience causes the opposite effect: we're always in a hurry and try to jam as much as we can into as little time as possible. As a result, there is little time for enjoying life or the scenery as we go.

In retrospect, the time I was privileged to have my children under my roof and under my wing is a blur and but a second in the eternal scheme. I was always hurrying to get them ready, to get them somewhere on time, to reach that next milestone or event. I'm afraid it was a lot of shortcuts and taking the fastest route. Now it is all but a faint memory of when they were little. Did I really stop and enjoy them enough? I would hope so, but I am not so sure.

I'm not sure of its origin, but I love the saying "We are human beings, not human doings." God gave us our lives and our children's lives to enjoy and savor. Yes, He expects us to work. That is essential, but it was not His intention that we live hurried, frenzied lives and not experience to the fullest this great journey He sent us on.

Slow down, stay in the right lane, take time to take in the scenery. You'll get there safely and in due time, and when you do, the memories will most certainly and wonderfully hold no regrets.

Prayer: *Father, help me to slow it down and appreciate every moment You give me and every breath I take. I ask for supernatural recall of any precious moment I may have forgotten. Amen.*

My Father's House

Love has been perfected among us in this: that we may have boldness
in the Day of Judgment; because as He is, so are we in this world.
1 John 4:17

I was dog-sitting for my daughter and son-in-law, and Sugar had a beauty-parlor appointment during that time. I dropped her off at the groomer and decided to stop at a local IHOP for breakfast and a little reading while I waited to pick her up. The location of this particular restaurant was across the street from a hospital and several medical clinics, so it would stand to reason that many of the breakfast clientele were on their way either to or from various doctor appointments.

I was absorbed in my book and, for a while, not aware of my surroundings, but at some point, a nearby conversation caught my attention. It was a lady and her elderly mother, just to my left; when I looked up, I could see that the mother was a cancer patient. The daughter was imploring her mother to eat. Now fully engaged in eavesdropping, I took note that the mother could not have weighed more than ninety pounds and looked gaunt and tired. From their conversation, I deduced that they were on their way to the next chemo treatment. The patient was not particularly motivated by this prospect, but the daughter was trying to be encouraging. "After today, we have eleven days before another one. Isn't that something to look forward to?" she said. The mother, I'm sure, was internally appreciative of the daughter's positivity, but she was unresponsive to her daughter's care and concern. She obviously didn't have the energy or spirit to show it.

To my right sat a young couple. They appeared to be arguing. He was sick but evidently still in the testing stages, and the doctors did not have a diagnosis yet. His wife was fussing at him because he had just admitted to her that he hadn't been completely honest with the doctor. He had withheld some key information that might have been helpful. They were sitting across from each other, he on a bench seat and she in a chair. They grew silent, and after they finished eating, the wife got up and joined her husband on the bench side, put her arm around him, laid her head on his shoulder, and sat in silence in this manner for quite some time. I was trying to hold back my tears and for some reason was not at all embarrassed that I was privy to such an intimate moment in the life of total strangers.

My attention turned across the aisle to a table directly in front of me. There was a short, sixtyish white woman sitting on the same side of her booth with a teenaged black boy. She was buttoning his shirt, and I then realized he was mentally handicapped. He was shaking and jerking heavily with some form of palsy and made loud, irritating sounds intermittently, as though he had a vocal tick. She spoon-fed him his breakfast between bites of her own. She was patient and loving, and he responded positively with the warmest, brightest, toothiest smile to each loving direction she gave him. There was a simple but explicit beauty in the scene. The caregiver loved her charge, and he loved her. My tears were no longer contained.

There was human drama unfolding all around me. I felt God's presence very suddenly and powerfully. I looked up and noticed a glass-paned partition that hung in the center of the restaurant. On it was an etched map of the eastern and western hemispheres. I felt Father was saying to me, "This is My world."

Where you find emotion of this depth, where you find suffering, where you find utter love and devotion, you find God. It all belongs to Him. The good, the bad, the ugly—He sees it all. It breaks His heart, and it brings Him joy. It is His, and He doesn't want us to miss it—miss seeing it, experiencing it. It is life with Him in its midst. Jesus experienced it all: the suffering of others and His own, and the love that is perfect, beautiful, and bittersweet. He took the memory of it with Him when He returned to the Father. Much of life on this earth is not clean, neat, and pretty, but He experienced it all to its fullest. It is all His. And so are we.

Prayer: *I don't ever want to be neglectful in including You in the good, the bad, and the ugly of my life. I thank You, Father, that You have a heart for Your people, and I am glad that I am one of them.*

A Season of Good-Byes

Let not your heart be troubled; you believe in God, believe also in Me.
In My Father's house are many mansions; if it were not so, I would
have told you. I go to prepare a place for you. And if I go and prepare a
place for you, I will come again and receive you to Myself;
that where I am, there you may be also.
John 14:1–3

Mike's grandfather, G-John, was ninety-four and well past the point of physically caring for himself and his wife, so it became necessary to move him out of his home of fifty years. It was a helpless feeling, watching a man whom we loved, admired, and respected walk away from a lifetime of memories, treasures, and the fruit of his lifelong labor, closing the door behind him, never to return.

We watched as he left behind a home where he had built two successful marriages, nursed a dying wife, and hosted a beautiful wedding reception for his only daughter and a wedding for us, along with many other memorable family gatherings. It was a home full of photographs and mementos, many of which were close to a hundred years old—a place of history, a place of happiness, a place of success in all areas of life. He had to say good-bye, and so did we. I don't know which was harder: our good-bye or witnessing him saying good-bye to it all.

Saying good-bye is a difficult reality of life, and there are plenty of opportunities to get good at it. We say good-bye to jobs, homes, loved ones, relationships, people in general, and our pets. We say good-bye to habits, ways of life, and traditions. We transition from one season of life to another, and as the dynamics change, as our lives change, we say good-bye to so much.

As Jesus breathed His last on the cross, I can only begin to imagine the despair that His family, close friends, and followers felt as they said good-bye. Their friend, their teacher, their Savior was gone. The joy that they had experienced in knowing Him, loving Him, gleaning His wisdom, and receiving His love was replaced with despair, loneliness, fear, and hopelessness. It was a good-bye they had hoped they would never have to say. The devastation, I'm sure, was immense. Then, on the third day, everything changed. The hopelessness was replaced with joy unspeakable as they realized that the good-bye had been only temporary.

I believe Father allows the good-byes of life so that we learn to let go and rely more on Him. He removes the sting of good-bye because He is always present, always comforting. Because of Jesus, all the truly devastating good-byes of our lives are temporary. He eases the heartache of separation with a hope of life eternal with the ones we love and, ultimately, with Him. In the midst of a lifetime of good-byes, we never have to say good-bye to Him, and that is the greatest hope and comfort of all.

Prayer: *I love this life you have given me, Lord, even with the many good-byes that I have had to say over the years. I'm thankful that You have been with me through each and every one of them and for the hope I have in You. Amen.*

The Empty House

*Do not lay up for yourselves treasures on earth, where moth and rust
destroy, and where thieves break in and steal; but lay up for yourselves
treasures in heaven, where neither moth nor rust destroys and where
thieves do not break in and steal. For where your treasure is,
there your heart will be also.*
Matthew 6:19–21

After the death of both of my parents, I had to sell their home and remove
all their belongings, furnishings, and, at the time, I thought, memories
too. I am an only child, so all the decisions of what to keep, what to throw
away, and what to give away or sell rested on my shoulders alone.

I found myself attaching the memory of my parents to each and every
little object, and it made it very hard for me to make those decisions. I
began to think that as I let go of each material object, I was letting go of
my parents, bit by bit. I kept thinking that if I held on to this or that, it
would help me to hang on to them. I felt like I was throwing my parents'
lives away.

I love collecting angels, and one day during this time, my eyes fell upon
one of my most cherished angel figurines in my bedroom. The thought
occurred to me, *If I died, what would I want my children to do with that
figurine?* The answer became crystal clear: it wouldn't matter to me.
When I pass away and move on to my home in heaven, I, like my parents,
will leave behind a lifetime of little trinkets that my children will have
to divide up or dispose of; they will have to decide which of my material belongings remind them the most of our time together and what is
most important to them. Personally, I would no longer have use for any
of these things.

I realized the memory of my parents was not dependent upon the material belongings left behind in their house. When they died, their home
became merely a house. They, and the love they shared with each other
and with me, were what made their house a home, not their belongings.
The real treasure, my parents, had left it all behind.

No doubt, God blesses us with material things. He gives us good things
to use and enjoy, but they are all temporary. The true, everlasting treasures are what we do with our lives and the lives of people we touch as

we walk this earth. Those are the things we take with us to heaven, and those are the things our loved ones will hang on to until they can be with us again. A kind of healing came when I realized the memories of my parents would last, but their stuff wouldn't, and that was finally okay with me.

My greatest treasure is Jesus, and He is an eternal one. My greatest memories of my parents are little snippets of time that are etched into my mind and heart: the sight of my mother running into my dad's arms the day he returned from Vietnam, my daddy unashamedly weeping openly at my wedding, the first time my mother held our beautiful little Sally in her arms, and my dad and I comforting each other on our first Mother's Day without Mama. These are my treasures. Father gave them to me; they are precious to me, and they are mine forever.

Prayer: *Memories are a wonderful gift and blessing, Father. I am eternally thankful to You for them all. Amen.*

My Unsung Hero

Honor your father and your mother, that your days may be long upon the land which the LORD your God is giving you.
Exodus 20:12

Note: *Mother's Day is always difficult for me. I have now experienced sixteen of them without my mama. The account below was written on the occasion of my first Mother's Day without her, and it is just as fresh, just as poignant for me as the day it was written.*

Mother's Day will be here soon, and for me, it will probably be the most difficult one I've ever celebrated. You see, this is the first time I won't be able to pay tribute to my mom in person. On March 11 of this year, my mom died very suddenly of a massive heart attack, with absolutely no warning whatsoever. I cannot begin to explain to you in human terms the devastation of this experience. However, I do think I can tell you in human terms how blessed I've been by this wonderful person and how grateful I am to the Lord God above for giving me such an awesome mother.

My mom has left behind a wonderful legacy of love, loyalty, faith, graciousness, sacrifice, and blessing. There is no way to measure the value of such things; all we can do is use them and pass them on. I hope I have done that and will continue to do that long into the future. There is a Bible verse that says, "Honor your father and your mother, that your days may be long upon the land which the LORD your God is giving you" (Exodus 20:12). I looked up the word *honor* in the dictionary, and the very first definition of it was this: "a good name or public esteem"; and the second one was "a showing of unmerited respect."

Mama always said, "*Every day* is Mother's Day when you're a mother." From her point of view, it was a privilege to be a mother and a grandmother. I can only hope it was true for her because I treated her with unmerited respect (although she was certainly worthy of it) and contributed to her good name and public esteem with my behavior. I wanted to honor her by sharing with you how special my mom was, so at the end of this day's writing, you will find an article that was written about her in the paper the day after she died. This is my tribute, my gift to her this Mother's Day.

A hero is someone who is admired for their achievements and noble qualities; an unsung hero is someone who achieves great things but goes unrecognized. I believe motherhood puts many of us into this second category. It certainly did for my mom.

Of course, Jesus is truly my hero. How often can I say that someone died for me? I am so grateful to Him for what He has done for both me and my mom, and because of His act of sacrifice, I can say without a doubt that she is having the best Mother's Day she has ever had. After all, she is with her mother, and she is with Jesus. As for me, I'll be with them all someday, and won't that be a sweet celebration? Happy Mother's Day, Mama.

"Unsung Hero" Dies on Day of Award
By Tom Normand
Staff writer

Jean Scott Lee, 64, nominated for one of the three 1999 Unsung Hero Awards from the Council of Community Services, died Thursday without knowing she was to be named a winner at the council's awards dinner that same night.

Mrs. Lee, financial director of New Horizons Corp., had been nominated for her behind-the-scenes volunteer efforts during her 25 years of employment by New Horizons.

But she suffered a heart attack at her Brentwood home and died at Southern Hills Medical Center. The organization had these words of praise for her at the event:

"She didn't realize when she began as a part-time substitute at New Horizons that she would be spending the next 25 years there wearing many hats.

"At that time, the agency had a handful of clients and a $36,000-a-year budget. Often, she pitched in to clean the toilets, run the machinery and even waited to deposit her paycheck when they hit rough times.

"Her effective leadership has grown our agency to serve nearly 200 adults with developmental disabilities with a $2 million budget. The staff and clients appreciate her caring heart and commitment to them all of these years."

Services will be at 2:30 p.m. today at Woodlawn Funeral Home. Burial will be in Woodlawn Memorial Park.

She was a native of Liberty, Tenn., and a daughter of the late Alton and Gertie Johnson Scott.

Mrs. Lee was a member of South End United Methodist Church.

Survivors include her husband, William J. Lee; a daughter, Judy L. Grenley, Old Hickory; three sisters, Joanne Voyles, Alexandria, La., Janet Nichols, Athens, Tenn., and Polly Manning, Brentwood; and two grandchildren.

The family asked that memorial contributions be made to New Horizons Corp., 5221 Harding Place, Nashville, Tenn. 37217.

Rejoice!

Philippians 4:4

This Little Light of Mine

Let your light so shine before men, that they may see your
good works and glorify your Father in heaven.
Matthew 5:16

Do you remember this line from that little song we sang in Sunday school: "This little light of mine / I'm gonna let it shine"? It came to my mind one day as I was sorting and putting away the Christmas decorations. I kept finding little flecks of glitter on the floor and on me, and no matter how hard I tried, I couldn't get them all to go away. I resigned myself to the fact that I (and the house) would be a little bit shiny for some time to come.

Then I realized that a little bit of glitter is a good thing. I didn't have to think of it as messy; it could be a reminder to let a little light shine through me in the coming year. New Year's was the time when I would resolve to be better, to stop something old, or to start something new. I always had the best of intentions, but most of the time, I ended up disappointing myself before the first week of January was over. I got tired of feeling like a failure, so I gave up on resolutions.

I decided to handle the New Year's thing a little differently. No more "lose weight, read the Bible more, and stop biting my nails" decisions. I decided to do one thing and one thing only: to allow myself to shine a little light, to be someone's glitter whenever the opportunity presented itself; to perform simple random acts of kindness, giving and forgiving, taking time to smile and brighten someone's day; and maybe just to remember that when someone else is behaving badly, it's probably because they are hurting inside and need a little grace from someone like me.

Father has put something shiny on the inside of us: His Spirit. If we are different, set apart, then it should show on the outside. He told us we should do so in Scripture. Through us, He wants to be a beacon to a dark and sad world. When Jesus walked this earth, He touched people's lives in a beautiful and everlasting way. He made a difference, and He continues to do that through His people when they cooperate. When we turn our focus onto impacting those around us for Him, our lights start to shine.

I've decided that every time I see something shiny or a little point of light somewhere, it's going to be my reminder to do something nice for someone else, no strings attached. Every year from now on, I want to make it a point to let my light shine—to be someone's glitter, a bright spot in the day of someone who needs it—and no doubt, when I need it, someone else will do the same for me.

Prayer: *I ask for opportunities, Father, to hug, serve, and speak kind words to the hurting for You, and may You be glorified through it. Amen.*

The Greatest Is Love

But now abide faith, hope, love, these three;
but the greatest of these is love.
1 Corinthians 13:13

Did you ever stop and think about how loosely we use the word *love*? "I *love* to go shopping," I *loved* that movie," "I *love* macaroni and cheese," "I *love* a good story," and "I just *love* my football team."

During Valentine's season, the word *love* is thrown around a lot. The dictionary includes nine different definitions of the word, most of which include the words *affection, attraction, attachment, admiration,* and *devotion,* and that which many of us regard as love, "a sentimental emotion or feeling."

The ancient Greeks painted a picture of love in several different ways linguistically, and these are depicted in the Scriptures: *eros* (passionate love), *philia* (brotherly friendship love), *storge* (familial love), and *agape* (sacrificial or the God kind of love).

Over the years, I have grown to connect the love God has for us with the love we have for our children. Though not perfect, as God's love is, the love we have for our children is the closest comparison in our human minds and hearts. Sure, we have great affection, sentimentality, and an emotional attachment to our kids, but we also give up so much, sacrifice so much, and would even die for them. That is the God kind of love.

In our day-to-day living, however, our love for our children and others can wane in ways that God's love doesn't. The Bible says that love is patient and kind. God patiently and in kindness waits on us to come to Him and patiently endures and forgives us as we grow up. He doesn't give up His patience or kindness; there is a never-ending supply.

We can't always say that about the love we have for our children. A day of messy diapers, a screaming child tugging on your leg for eight straight hours, or the rolling eyes of an indignant teenager can cause you to lose your spirituality fairly quickly and gives you pause to think again about this wonderful parenting thing.

But this *agape* love, God's love, the love that we easily relate to, is summed up as an action word, a verb. It says, "I may not feel it, but I do it anyway." It's really easy to go out and buy a sentimental card and a box of chocolates, or help the kids sign the cute little cartoon cards they bring to school every Valentine's Day. Those are all perfectly nice and wonderful things, but real love, *agape* love, challenges us to become instruments of self-sacrifice, no matter how we feel at the moment.

I'm sure if we had the opportunity to ask Him, Jesus would most certainly have said He didn't "feel" like going to the cross on our behalf, and it certainly wasn't convenient. But He did it because of *agape* love. It was His sacrificial response to the need of mankind, and His reaction was demonstrative, excruciatingly painful, and perfect. So the next time the kids, the spouse, or the neighbors start to drive you a little crazy, just think of Jesus and say, "I love you anyway, even if I don't feel like it." Oh, and it's okay to really, really, really *like* your macaroni and cheese.

Prayer: *Lord, help me to show Your love to others. Give me opportunities to demonstrate Your agape love to those who need it most. Amen.*

The Holy Week Experience

I am the resurrection and the life. He who believes in Me,
though he may die, he shall live.
John 11:25

Holy Week brings back powerful childhood memories: shopping at Sears or Castner Knott for pastel ruffled dresses and white patent-leather Mary Janes, not to forget the matching purse and hat and the all-important white cardigan sweater to top off the perfect Easter outfit. A begrudging little brother acquiesced to a tie and shirt that coordinated with the family's Easter ensemble and new stiff leather shoes that he would complain about every Sunday throughout the summer.

Dyeing Easter eggs—remember those old PAAS egg-dyeing kits, the smell of vinegar and boiled eggs? The colors were so bright, eye candy after the dullness of a long winter. And what about singing old Easter favorites, like "Easter Parade" or "Here Comes Peter Cottontail"? The forsythia, redbuds, Bradford pears, and tulip trees lit up the sky in an array of bright colors, and the weather warmed just enough to tease you into going outside without a jacket.

For me, the week really began with Palm Sunday at church and the Easter-egg hunt afterward. Roadside stands were stocked with live chicks and bunnies that were fun to pet, but no matter how much I begged, I could never bring one home. Good Friday was usually somber and quiet; there was no school, and if the weather permitted, we could play outside for a while. Clover was blooming, and we would lie on the hillside and make crowns from the white flowers, a sad reminder of another crown made of thorns.

Mother was baking, preparing for Sunday. Saturday night all my brand-new Easter clothing was laid out over a bedroom chair, and then Mom rolled my hair in those pink spongy rollers. With the pain of the rollers and the excited anticipation of the Easter Bunny, I could hardly sleep at all on Saturday night. Long before the sun was up, the smell of coffee, bacon, and cinnamon rolls awakened me, and I ran to the living room to find a brightly colored basket filled with candy and toys and a sweet little stuffed bunny that would be difficult to part with when I went off to church.

Easter sunrise service was almost mystical as the sun rose to an a cappella rendition of "Up from the Grave He Arose." After services, it was off to Grandmother's for a delicious ham dinner, topped off with a white fluffy coconut cake decorated with jelly beans, and showing off all the Easter Bunny loot to the cousins.

At Easter time, the world is coming back to life from its winter slumber. It is a natural revival. As we make wonderful Easter memories, we must be mindful that just as the natural world is brought back to life around us, God has done the same for us. We are resurrected spirits in Him. As we celebrate His resurrection, we also celebrate ours.

Does your heart feel open to Him, to His Spirit? Do you feel the fresh vitality of the resurrected Jesus in your daily life? If not, tell Him. Pray for that sense of renewal to come upon you the way spring comes upon the world. We all need to feel that tender newness that only Jesus can bring, and He wants to give it to you. It is so much better than a new dress and a basket of eggs. Happy Resurrection Day!

Prayer: *Because of Your sacrifice, Lord, every day is Resurrection Day. On the days I feel blue, old, and tired, please help me to remember this wonderful truth. Amen.*

A Really Bad Day

For as by one man's disobedience many were made sinners, so also by one Man's obedience many will be made righteous.
Romans 5:19

Did you ever have a bad day? No matter what the cause—oversleeping or no sleeping, burning breakfast, dropping everything you touch, hundreds of telemarketers calling your house, screaming kids, grouchy spouses, ATMs that won't give you your money, broken water heaters, or overflowing toilets—it's all bad, I know. In the normal course of life, we rarely have a truly bad day, but let me tell you about a day that was truly bad.

You begin the day battered and bruised because you were whipped and beaten all night long, so much so that you have no skin or muscle left on your back. Breakfast? It is not offered, and besides, you have no appetite. You're lying on a stone floor, cold and nearly naked, and you feel weak, sick, and light-headed. Later, as you are led outdoors, throngs of people are crying, screaming, and yelling at you and calling you terrible names as they spit on you. Then you are forced to make a long walk uphill, carrying a heavy, splintered beam on your raw and bleeding back. Your feet and legs give way beneath the weight of the beam, and though a kind soul offers you help, the uphill trek is still brutal.

When you reach the top of the hill, rough and uncaring soldiers shove you down onto the beam and drive large nails through your hands and feet to confine you to the crossbeam and post. The pain is unbearable, yet you endure it anyway. As you are lifted high into the air, the weight of your body sags downward, pulling and straining against the nails in your hands and feet. Now every breath is a struggle as you press downward on your feet to lift your body, forcing air into your lungs and scraping your wounded, torn, and raw back against the rough wood each time you take a breath. Again and again you repeat this process just to stay alive.

The agony and humiliation are beyond belief. You feel like your body is coming apart, and you want to die to stop the pain, but there is more work to do. Finally, there comes a deep, sharp pain in your side where a sword has been thrust. You can't see it, but you feel the fluids gushing rapidly from your body. You're dehydrated, thirsty, and your head is pounding.

LITTLE PARABLES OF LIFE

Oh, for blessed relief from the excruciating pain, and it only comes by death after six long hours upon this cross.

The irony of this really bad day is that you didn't deserve a thing that happened to you in the last twenty-four hours. You're innocent—guiltless. But you had to suffer this for the sake of someone who *is* guilty. During all the hours of suffering, unseen by the soldiers and other witnesses, an invisible kind of suffering was taking place. Every sin that had ever been committed in the past, every sin being committed today, and every sin ever to be committed in the future was striking your body, soul, and spirit. You took in so much sin that you became sin. Every sinful thought, every evil deed, every abuse, every foul thing that was ever thought, said, or committed by a human being throughout the entire history of the world, from beginning to end, was nailed to the cross with you, through you, and in you, assaulting your perfection and innocence. The unfairness of it all is beyond staggering, and the underlying grace of it, beyond measure.

Now that's a really bad day, yet amazingly we call it "Good" Friday. So why is it good? The good news is that the *you* on this bad day was Jesus. He took your place, and you didn't have to pay the debt you owed. He paid it for you. The really good news is that because He was perfect and knew no sin of His own, death had no hold on Him, no power over Him. He rose again, and He is alive! And that makes it a really good day.

Prayer: *Open unbelieving eyes and ears, Father, to the grand plan that You fashioned to save the world You love. I rejoice in Jesus' resurrection, and I thank You for the incredible sacrifice of Your Son. Amen.*

My Mother's Hands

And let the beauty of the Lord our God be upon us, and establish the work of our hands for us; yes, establish the work of our hands.
Psalm 90:17

Time passes quickly. The years come and go. Holidays, celebrations, and milestones also come and go. It seems as though you barely get the Christmas decorations put away each year and then they are back out again. Mother's Day is a marker for me; it's an important day. I've experienced many Mother's Days as a mother: more than thirty of them now, and many Mother's Days without a mother, more than fifteen of them now. I am nearing the age that my mother was when she passed away, and the speed with which time is passing I find unbelievable.

Besides the clock ticking and the calendar pages flipping by at warp speed, other changes occur with this speedy passage of time. The body makes some startling changes. For instance, you acquire a level of eyesight that requires reading glasses and affords you the ability to miss some things that you once thought were important. Mercifully, you no longer notice the dust on your plants, the cobwebs in your corners, the laugh lines around your eyes, and other decidedly insignificant details of life that disappear with the loss of 20/20 vision and the well-seasoned ability to prioritize.

One day, while washing a few dishes with my reading glasses on, I looked down and caught a glimpse of my mother's hands in the dishwater. Now, my hands are far from being as beautiful as hers were. My mother's hands were always beautifully manicured, soft and smooth, but just as beautiful from within as without. They had a soft, tender, loving touch. They spoke a language of kindness and unconditional acceptance to anyone who welcomed their caress. My mother's touch evoked in me a flood of security and well-being so deep and powerful that even now, years since I last felt it, the mere memory of it comforts me down to my soul.

They were the hands of a good mother, and there they were, like a ghost in my dishwater. All at once I was surprised and honored that I had her hands. They were not yet wrinkled, but the taut silkiness of my youth had disappeared from them. They looked as though they had lived the ups and downs of life. Now they have experience and inner strength. They have worked, loved, and held children. They have guided, disciplined, and dried both my own tears and those of others. They have helped to heal hearts, prayed many prayers, and without embarrassment reached toward the heavens in praise of God. I was struck in that moment that my tender youth really was behind me, but a new, better tenderness had replaced it, and I welcomed it.

God is not just a father to us. After my mother passed away, I was comforted when I realized that He is all the things a good mother is as well. Jesus' hands tell the tale: they were worn, weathered, strong, hardworking, kind, loving, and, above all else, self-sacrificing. He allowed them to be pierced and scarred for us. Just as He held Himself up on the cross with those pierced hands to get the job done, He also holds us up through our hurts and our pain.

As a Christian, it has been my hope, my goal, to become as much like Him as possible. He is my plumb line and my example, so my desire, my resolve for my future, is that someday I'll look down and will see not only the hands of my mother, but those of my heavenly Father as well.

Prayer: *Thank You, Lord, for Your loving touches. They cannot be seen with the eyes, but they can be felt with the heart. They have been my healing and my salvation, and I am grateful for every one of them. Amen.*

Her Joy Remains

Let your father and your mother be glad,
and let her who bore you rejoice.
Proverbs 23:25

She was overjoyed when you appeared on this planet, and her life was never the same. She walked the floor with you and lay on the floor by your crib to hopefully and expectantly listen for your continued breathing. And her joy did not diminish.

She nourished you from her own body, stroked your cheek, and deeply inhaled the sweet baby aroma from the top of your little head. She kissed your toes, patted your "tushie," changed your diaper, and wiped every part of you clean.

She shed tears of happiness at the thought of you and learned what true fear was because of you. Her heart ached as you grew up and away from her, yet lovingly she let you go. And in her grief, the joy of motherhood remained. You changed her life, and she wouldn't have it any other way.

At some point in life for most of us, we did not look at her in such an honorable way. In her human nature, she may have failed us or at least appeared to do so. I do not believe there are bad mothers—just hurt ones. If she did fail us, she knew it, and that, too, was a grief only a mother could bear. We learned this when we ourselves became mothers; only then could we understand and forgive her.

Mommy, Mama, Mom, Mother—*who* she is, is *what* she is. All that you are, you owe to her. To her, you are everything. Even if she has departed this world, none of that has changed. She is and always will be "Mother."

I now experience Mother's Day each year without my mother. But I always spend at least part of the day with my children as they celebrate their mother, and together, we remember my mom and speak of her with honor. We know in our hearts that she is smiling and that her joy, after all this time, still remains.

Prayer: *Having a mother such as mine and becoming a mother myself have been my privilege. Thank You for bestowing these honors and the joy that they bring upon me, Lord. Amen.*

No "Daddy Issues" Here

But as many as received Him, to them He gave the right to become children of God, to those who believe in His name: who were born, not of blood, nor of the will of the flesh, nor of the will of man, but of God.
John 1:12–13

We tend to take them for granted—dads. They mow the lawn, take out the trash, make sure the car is washed and has oil, and intimidate the boyfriend at the front door. Unfortunately, however, the real value of a dad is often overlooked until we no longer have one. A good dad is a good husband, and a good husband makes Mama happy. And you know what they say about that. . . .

A good dad instills self-confidence in his children by encouraging them to take risks, to capitalize on their successes, and to view their failures as stepping-stones to the next achievement. A good dad teaches his daughter how she should be treated by a man, and his son how to treat a woman. A good dad has big shoulders for his children to ride on and to cry on. A good dad has that "look" that sets his kids on the straight and narrow without a word being spoken. A good dad teaches his kids to laugh at themselves, and those lessons usually come on family vacations when nothing goes right. Still, we end up holding the experience as a dear memory forever. A good dad cherishes his kids and finds incredible joy in the grandchildren at his feet.

Jesus called God "Abba." A close translation of this word is "Father." It is honorable and implies respect, confidence, and a reverential intimacy. It suggests a relationship that allows approach with a bold humility. Because of Jesus, we have been adopted into His family, and we can also call Him "Father." When I began to think of Him in this way, my relationship with Him changed. It became real and personal.

As a counselor, on many occasions I have been privy to the negative experiences of those with "daddy issues." Abandonment is the most common thread among them, physically, emotionally, or spiritually. Dads are human; they aren't perfect. Many of them have also experienced abandonment, hurt, and abuse. It's not an excuse for them to pass that on to their children, but it does help us to understand them better. Thankfully, we do have a Father who does not abandon, does not abuse, and does not make mistakes with us. He is our Abba, our heavenly Father. He's a good dad, and an intimate, personal relationship with Him brings us to a place of healing in those areas where our human fathers unfortunately missed the mark.

We all remember and think of our dads differently, but what I know is this: they usually do the best they can, and they do it because they love us first and themselves last. If for some reason they aren't remembered as good dads, it is because they didn't have one themselves. Please don't wait for the next Father's Day to come around, take time today to remember your father fondly. Call him if you can, and forgive him if it is needed. You'll feel better if you do.

Prayer: *Father, help us to see our dads the way You see them. Give us the eyes of Christ where they are concerned and the strength to forgive where it is needed. Amen.*

Remember to Laugh

A merry heart does good, like medicine,
but a broken spirit dries the bones.
Proverbs 17:22

There are a lot of serious moments in life, times that are stressful, difficult, and sometimes traumatic. I've had a lot of those moments in my life, but in thinking of those times now, in retrospect I've discovered something interesting. Even in the darkest, saddest, or most serious moments of my life, I can look back and remember some humorous aspect or occurrence that actually helped me through it.

At my wedding, my father was so overcome with emotion that my mother had to physically pull him from the room, and throughout our vows, we could hear him weeping and bellowing loudly in the next room. The pastor who officiated had had his wisdom teeth extracted that week and still had cotton packing in his mouth. Between the cotton packing and the angst on the other side of the wall, we could barely hear the vows to repeat them. On top of all that, Mike said, "With this *wing*, I thee wed." We laughed a little then, and at the thought of it all now, it brings quite a chuckle.

I admit to being extremely mean and surly toward my husband during labor and childbirth. At the time, I'm sure it left him wondering, what was this thing he had married? Labor and delivery are not humorous, especially when you are the one giving birth. Even then, I smiled at the look on Mike's face and how awkward he looked dressed in operating room garb, trying to work the camera while keeping a safe distance from this woman who wanted to kill him. I still smile at the thought. Without all the pain and irritation, I find it all pretty hilarious now.

When my mother passed away, a favorite aunt of mine was discovered "sharing" her knee- replacement scars in another room of the funeral home. This required lifting her skirt to an uncomfortable height to show anyone of some familiar acquaintance who was either interested or cared to compare hers with their own scars. It sounds very irreverent, but it truly was a brief moment of hilarity that was a little piece of grace that got me through a really dark time.

Laughter is a gift from God. I like to think of it as the music of the soul. I have no doubt that Jesus did it a lot when He walked this earth. I picture Him laughing at Peter and all of his impetuous ways or with the little children as they came to Him for a blessing. I think of Him laughing out loud with delight as the loaves and fishes were divided, increased, and fed the multitudes. I'm sure He good-naturedly laughed a little at Zacchaeus up in that tree, who was hoping to catch a glimpse of Jesus as He passed by, knowing full well how He was about to bless him. As the reality of the cross became apparent, I hope He was able to smile a little, at least inwardly, at the thought of the eternal reward that was to come afterward. Maybe that thought helped Him through it.

It's good to laugh; it's healthy. It makes life more joyful and helps us get through the tough times. Laughter is known to lower the blood pressure; it also releases brain chemistry that makes us feel better and helps to heal us. It lightens the mood when things are awkward and when we learn to laugh at ourselves, can make us feel a little less self-conscious. It can make a marriage better and parenting less stressful. It's best done in the company of friends, and often.

Life can be serious, but laughter gets us through. Laughter is a gift from above and a gift we give to each other. I hope every day you will let your soul sing a little, give this gift to yourself, and then pass it along to someone else who could use a little laughter too.

Prayer: *All Your gifts are wonderful, Father. Laughter is one of my favorites. Thank You for the times that You sent a lighter moment so that a little humor could see me through. Amen.*

Where Are the Fireworks?

I will lift up my eyes to the hills—from whence comes my help?
My help comes from the LORD, who made heaven and earth.
Psalm 121:1–2

Boom. Boom. Crackle. Fizzle. Oooh. Ahhh. You know what that is—fireworks! To me, they are a phenomenon. I don't understand how they work—I just know they do. There are only a few times in the year when we see them, and when we do, we are awestruck and celebrating something.

When I was little, I was afraid of fireworks. They made no sense to my childish mind. I was positive the fire would fall right on me; it seemed so much closer than it actually was, and everything was too big and too loud. As a child, I had no concept of the nature of fireworks, so the fear kept me at a distance, usually hiding behind my daddy or in the backseat of the car. To this day, I find fireworks surreal and a little unnerving, but their power is amazing and stimulating, and their beauty a feast for the eyes.

Ezekiel also witnessed something spectacular and amazing, so much so that his mind could not conceive of it. He had to describe what he saw by what he knew; he likened it to things that were familiar to him. His descriptions include the likeness of fire, colors of amber, sapphire stones, and the rainbow. He mentions the likeness of the glory of the Lord. It was in his human mind, truly indescribable. In the midst of this beauty, wonder, and dramatic activity, God spoke to him. I think it is safe to say that He got Ezekiel's attention (Ezekiel 1–2).

There are other eyewitness accounts in Scripture where the people of God looked up and saw something indescribable, surreal, and miraculous. The children of Israel followed a continuous pillar of cloud by day and of fire by night to lead the way as they departed Egypt and moved through the wilderness (Exodus 13:20–23). At the birth of Jesus, the angel of the Lord and a heavenly host appeared to the simple shepherds watching over their flocks in the dead of night (Luke 2:8–14). And the disciples were privileged to watch and marvel as the transfigured Jesus ascended into heaven (Luke 24:50–53).

With our modern, high-tech, scientifically savvy ways, we like to think that we are no longer a primitive, simpleminded people. We understand more, we can explain more, and we are too sophisticated to believe in visions and angelic sightings. However, there might come a time when we are proven wrong. God's ways are higher than ours, and He is the one who created science, after all.

The Scriptures mention another sighting from above that all will partake of, including those who do not believe. It will be surreal, spectacular, indescribable, and unlike anything our human eyes have ever witnessed. We will look up and see Jesus return in the clouds (Mark 13:26–27). He will return to earth victoriously, as a mighty warrior coming to claim that which is rightfully His—us.

It could happen in your lifetime, so keep looking up. When you see it, it will certainly get your attention, and there will be no other explanation. It will be time to celebrate, and if any of us is even able to utter a sound, you might hear an *ooh* and an *ahhh* or two from the crowd.

Prayer: *Father, my eyes have never witnessed a pillar of fire from above, an angel descending from heaven, or the heavenly host proclaiming Your glory, but the evidence of Your existence is all around me. I know You are real and that in Your due time, we all will see how amazing and spectacular You are. Amen.*

No Rest for the Weary

Come to Me, all you who labor and are heavy laden,
and I will give you rest.
Matthew 11:28

Labor Day is kind of an enigma in the scheme of holidays. It's not a remembrance of a specific event in history or a high holy day. It's more of a tradition, an American one that pays tribute to American workers and their achievements. For many, it marks the end of summer and return to school, and the entrance of fall activity and the coming holidays. We associate it with getting together with family and friends for one last romp in the lake or the pool and eating barbecue and corn on the cob. For most, it's another paid day off from work.

In my mind, *labor* is a depiction of things like giving birth, digging ditches, lifting heavy objects, and exerting an inordinate amount of energy to the point of complete and utter depletion. It's a description of something physically taxing. I don't often connect the word *labor* with typing on a computer, studying a spreadsheet, or talking on the phone. Yet those of us who do these things for a living do get tired and worn-out and weary. We get mind weary. It's a different kind of tired, and we, too, need to rest.

Jesus understood fatigue and weariness. He walked everywhere. There were no taxicabs in Judea in His day. He walked among mobs of people who pressed in to Him as He moved about. They wanted a look, a touch, a word from the Master. He had to climb hills to get to a place where they weren't all over Him and where they could see and hear Him.

Jesus spent time in the desert without food. He walked on water to catch up with the guys. Often He had to leave town quickly to avoid those trying to kill Him. He had to settle petty arguments, touch the sick and afflicted, and make dead people get up. He was busy, constantly interrupted, intruded upon, called upon, and consumed by the needs of those around Him. So even Jesus, our Lord and Savior, "God with us," got tired, physically, mentally, and spiritually. The Scriptures tell us that He found time to get away from people to pray and be with the Father (Mark 1:35). This was necessary for Him to keep going, and He was able to give more of Himself because of it.

In comparison to the life He led, we've got it pretty easy. We get a fifteen-minute break here, a thirty-minute break there; we get lunch hours, five-day workweeks, and two days off each week. We have the major holidays off, two weeks of vacation every year, and sick days and personal days when we need them. Then we get Labor Day to commemorate all of our . . . work.

Jesus told us to come to Him and He would give us rest. He understands the need, and He takes care of it. So, from now on, when you get tired, really tired, find a quiet place and take your need to Him. Give it to Him and have a rest from your labor.

Prayer: *The busyness of life exhausts me, Father. But in You, Lord, I always find perfect rest. Amen.*

A Most Memorable Feast

*Behold, I stand at the door and knock. If anyone hears My voice
and opens the door, I will come in to him and
dine with him, and he with Me.*
Revelation 3:20

When the holiday season is ushered in at Thanksgiving, it becomes what I call the "eating season," a season of feasting. One of my husband's most endearing and generous qualities that shows up at this time of year is that he always waits to be the last one served at dinner. No matter if we are serving immediate or extended family or a house full of guests, he hangs behind and waits. It gives him great pleasure in making sure everyone else has enough on their plates for a more than satisfying meal. I love that about him.

The dictionary defines a *feast* as "an elaborate meal" or "something that gives unusual or abundant pleasure." As you can see, the word *feast* elevates a meal to a lofty place where it becomes elaborate and abundant. If you ever have the opportunity to study feasts in the Scriptures, you will very quickly see that there were quite a few of them in the Hebrew tradition. There are many Christian folks who will argue that the feasts were never to cease but were to continue; those traditions and observances were to continue past the cross. Either way, it doesn't matter to me. I just like to eat!

In everything Jesus does, He completes. He fulfilled the Scriptures, including the feasts. He *is* the feast, our feast. He is our Passover (the feast of salvation); He is our Bread of Life (the Feast of Unleavened Bread); He is our atonement (Yom Kippur). There are seven feasts in total, and all of them point to Jesus, to His perfection and to the good news of His suffering, death, and resurrection, and the resulting provision of our eternal life.

Because of this good news, He is able to extend to us a very special invitation. He, Jesus, King of Kings and Lord of Lords, the only begotten Son of the almighty God of the universe, and the fulfillment of all the feasts, extends to us—just the regular folks—this invitation:

Behold, I stand at the door and knock. If anyone hears My voice and opens the door, I will come in to him and dine with him, and He with Me. To him who overcomes I will grant to sit with Me on My throne, as I also overcame and sat down with My Father on His throne.
Revelation 3:20–21

Not only does He invite us to an elaborate, abundant dinner, but He also invites us to sit on the throne with Him. He's offering us the best chair at His table. When I think of dining with Jesus, I envision Him waiting until everyone else has had the opportunity to partake. Jesus waits at His banqueting table; He wants us all to have our fill, and He wants us all to experience, not only the elaborate, abundant banquet, but His wonderful presence and great joy at our being with Him there. And *that* is something to feast on!

Prayer: *It amazes me, Father, that You desire to fellowship and eat with me, one of the regular folks. May I be eternally thankful for every provision You have made to make this so in my life. Amen.*

How Thankful We Are

Thanks be to God for His indescribable gift!
2 Corinthians 9:15

A long time ago, I knew a family at church, a rather large family, who very rarely had a surplus of food to eat. Yet every time they sat down to a meal together, whether it was beans and cornbread, meat and potatoes, or just cereal, they held hands and said in unison, "How thankful we are! How thankful we are! How thankful we are!" Then they said their blessing and enjoyed their meal together. And you know what? They truly were thankful.

It shames me to know that I, who always have plenty to eat, more than adequate shelter, a beautiful family, many wonderful friends, excellent health, and, most importantly, an *awesome* God, would let a single day go by without being truly and utterly thankful. I think of this at Thanksgiving—a day set aside for just this purpose, and yet, how many Thanksgivings come and go without us taking time to really be thankful?

Most Thanksgiving mornings, we get up early to start cooking, run to the store for forgotten or misplaced items, and pack up the car in a mad rush to get where we are going. Somebody is probably getting angry and testy because we are late. Then, finally, we sit down to a beautiful meal, with football games blaring in the background, and say a quick prayer of thanks. We never stop to seriously and purposefully consider all the many blessings we have and should be thankful for.

Thanksgiving is and should be a holy day, considering to whom we are being thankful. The Bible says, "Enter into His gates with thanksgiving, and into His courts with praise. Be thankful to Him, and bless His name" (Psalm 100:4). Maybe if we take time to mindfully consider Him and enter in with thanksgiving, then maybe we will experience the holiday to its fullest and receive a little blessing from the One who *is* our feast, our reason to give thanks, and who gives us all things to enjoy.

Prayer: *I say many "thank You's" to You, Father. I pray that each one is said from my heart with true sincerity and gratitude and not from habit or because it happens to be a day I'm expected to do so. What You have done for me and what You have given me are beyond measure. Amen.*

The Thankful Heart

That I may proclaim with the voice of thanksgiving,
and tell of all Your wondrous works.
Psalm 26:7

I received a praise report and prayer update about a family who had been struggling with near-terminal health issues for quite some time and was reminded of just how good I have it and, more importantly, how very little I show my gratitude.

My husband and I are able-bodied, in better health than most, active. We are gainfully employed, enjoy our work, and are pretty good at our jobs. After thirty-seven years together, we are in love, relish our time together, and miss each other when we are apart. Our children are independent, responsible, talented adults. They, too, have been lucky in love and are good at their work. We all live in a country where we are free to move about at will, have everything we need at our disposal, and can pursue happiness and speak our minds. In comparison to most of the world, we are extremely blessed—blessed beyond comprehension and words. For this reason and many others, I am obligated to cultivate a thankful heart.

The thankful heart finds joy in the simple things: being able to hear the birds sing or a child's laughter; the ability to watch a sunset, climb stairs, or pick up a penny off the ground; and in the rich fragrance of a beautiful rose or brewing coffee and frying bacon. The thankful heart appreciates the beauty of true friendship and family, people it can count on.

The thankful heart looks forward and upward, does not harbor the pain of the past, and looks for the best in everyone. The thankful heart is not irritated when it does not get its own way and accepts that every *no* means a better *yes* later on. In the face of tragedy, the thankful heart says, "There, but for the grace of God, go I." The thankful heart loves better, listens better, lives better. An attitude of gratitude can change everything.

Is your heart thankful today? If not, just say those two little words to a stranger, to a friend, to your mate, and to your God today, and you'll be feeling thankful soon.

Prayer: *Thank You, Father, for my husband and family, my friends, my health, and most of all for Jesus. No matter what my circumstances, I pray that I will always demonstrate my gratitude to the world and in the process bring glory to You. Amen.*

The Christmas Spirit

*And she will bring forth a Son, and you shall call His name Jesus,
for He will save His people from their sins.*
Matthew 1:21

Remember that excited anticipation of Christmas coming, how the month of December seemed to tick by in slow motion as you turned the square on your Advent calendar each day? Do you remember that tickle you got in the back of your throat when you heard the first "Silent Night" rendition of the year? Then, there was the hope of snow on Christmas Eve, looking forward to visits with family and friends, putting up the tree and other Christmas decorations, and setting baby Jesus in His rightful place in the family nativity set. Many of these experiences, as well as the remembrance of them, evoke a feeling of what we often call the "Christmas spirit."

Not everyone has happy Christmas experiences or memories. Many people go to such great lengths to avoid any aspect of the Christmas season that even Ebenezer Scrooge would not be able to compete. Some unfortunate souls become so depressed at this time of year that they take their own lives. There is an expectation that something special should be happening; warm fuzzy feelings should be felt; people should take notice, be kinder, more loving. When it does not happen, it feels lonely and vastly empty.

It seems that whatever mankind gets its hands on, it ruins. I could go on and on here about the commercialization of Christmas, but that's a dead horse we don't need to beat. I think most folks would agree that Christmas is not the same as it used to be. I'm sure I don't need to remind you of the real meaning of Christmas, either: to ask you to turn your thoughts and hearts back to a stable in Bethlehem and a little baby laid in a manger on a cold winter night. We, or at least most of us, know the Christmas story. We know it's not about Santa Claus and reindeer and trees and presents. We know that it is a reminder of the One who came as a humble child in a humble place to save a dying world.

The Christmas spirit is really an attitude of the heart. If you have Jesus, every day can be a celebration, every day is a blessing, and every day is an opportunity for kindness and love. When you have Jesus, you can have peace and goodwill every day. You just have to remember it and put it into operation. It happens when you turn your attention off yourself and onto others, for it's in the giving, not the receiving, that the Christmas spirit resides.

When you celebrate Christmas this year, I hope you find the Christmas spirit. I hope it overtakes you with love and compassion and giving to others. I hope you will remember that Jesus is not just the reason for the season, but the reason for everything.

Prayer: *I love everything about Christmas, Lord. But more than anything, I love You. Thank You for the precious and perfect gift of Yourself. Amen.*

Going Home

*For our citizenship is in heaven, from which we also eagerly wait
for the Savior, the Lord Jesus Christ, who will transform our lowly
body that it may be conformed to His glorious body, according to
the working by which He is able even to subdue all things to Himself.*
Philippians 3:20–21

Christmastime is the time of year when we all think of going home—you know, back to Mother's house for Christmas. It reminds me of a line from an old bluegrass Christmas song: "Christmas time's a-comin', and I'll be going home"; or from another old favorite, "I'll be home for Christmas." There's just something about Christmas that makes us want to go home, wherever that is.

One Christmas our son, Will, received two parakeets as presents. That following spring, one of them got loose in the front yard and flew into the trees. Just like with us, to that parakeet, home was the place where he was safe, well fed, and had a familiar, loving voice to make him feel at home. For him, that place of safety and security was his cage—home.

Will was heartbroken and frantic, so my husband was determined to lure the bird back into his home. He left the female in the cage as an enticement and barricaded her so she could not get out. Then he placed the open cage in the tree near the little escapee. Mike and our son stood watching for hours, hoping the little guy would just get hungry enough or lonely enough to go back into the cage. There were several moments during that time when we thought we would be successful, but unfortunately, it never happened. Shortly after dark, the bird flew off, and we never saw him again.

Earth is just a stopover place for us. It is not really home. God has designed a very special place for all of us to go home to—heaven. When He sent Jesus to earth, His purpose was to make a way for all who believe in Jesus to go home. I can only imagine Jesus waiting, tirelessly watching to see if we will decide to go home. It is up to us, after all. Should we fly off in another direction, no one else can replace us in Jesus' eyes. We are unique and special to Him, and it breaks His heart when we don't choose His way.

When Jesus came, it became an option, an opportunity, for us to choose to go home. When we do, when we choose Him and the wonderful home He has prepared for us in heaven, no Christmas celebration on earth can compare to the celebration all of heaven enjoys for our sakes.

Prayer: *What a blessing and what a privilege it is, Lord, to be able to choose You, to choose life eternal with You in a place that is far beyond my human imagination—my eternal home, heaven. Amen.*

Happy Birthday, Jesus!

Therefore, whether you eat or drink, or whatever you do,
do all to the glory of God.
1 Corinthians 10:31

Christmas is my very favorite time of the year. It's a time to return to your childhood, to revisit the season with the eyes of a child, to experience the wonder and magic of it all. It is a time to observe traditions with family and friends. When my children were growing up, there were several Christmas traditions that we observed and remember fondly to this day.

The children took turns putting the angel on the top of the tree each year. On the even- numbered years, Sally would place it, and on the odd-numbered years, it was Will's turn —both, of course, with their daddy's help. Setting up our little homemade nativity scene was also a favorite, and of course, arguments ensued over who would put baby Jesus in the manger. Out of the protest arose another tradition. Every year Will would hide the baby from Sally, and it became a game for the family to find baby Jesus so we could set Him in His rightful place.

For a few years, we took the children on a day hike on Christmas Eve day. If I remember correctly, it was because the year before our first outing like this, the children absolutely would not or could not go to sleep on Christmas Eve. Necessity being the mother of invention, we took to day hiking in the cold to get them good and tired and hopefully off to sleep early. They didn't think too much of this little tradition, however, and after a few years, it waned. They figured out that if they would go to bed and go to sleep, no Arctic hikes would be necessary. They both consider themselves "permanently damaged" from this abuse of parental power, and we still have a good laugh about it every Christmas.

Another tradition that Mike and I still enjoy is looking at Christmas lights. When the kids were little, we'd bundle them up and tour the nearby neighborhoods at night. We'd just drive around looking at the beautiful lights, looking forward to steaming cups of hot chocolate when we arrived back home.

At church every year, we would have a birthday party for Jesus in the children's department, complete with cake, decorations, and a rousing rendition of "Happy Birthday to You" sung in unison and with great joy and youthful glee to the unseen recipient of this honor. It was sweet, oh so sweet.

My very favorite memory of a family Christmas tradition is reading the story of Jesus' birth to our little ones before bedtime. They would listen with wide-eyed wonder as the account of Joseph, Mary, baby Jesus, the shepherds, and wise men unfolded. It truly is a wondrous story, and seeing their reaction to it was priceless.

Traditions are important. They bind us together. They make our families unique and special, and they produce precious memories that we cherish. There are a lot of Christians who no longer celebrate Christmas in the traditional way; they feel it is irreverent, not authentic. That's fine. I am no judge of another's conscience—to each his own. To me, the way we celebrate—the *when*, *where*, and *how*—are not important. It's the fact that we remember what a gift Jesus is to us and that we take time to honor His coming. It's important that we reverence who He is and acknowledge that He is the tie that binds. So whenever it is, however it is, I feel there is no offense in saying to Him, "Happy birthday, Lord. I'm glad You came."

Prayer: *Father, mercy says I deserve punishment, but instead You gave me grace. Grace says I don't deserve You, but You gave Yourself for me anyway, just because You love me. May every day be a celebration of Your loving gift to me and to all mankind. Amen.*

Riding on Daddy's Shoulders

The beloved of the LORD shall dwell in safety by Him, who shelters him all the day long; and he shall dwell between His shoulders.
Deuteronomy 33:12

It was a very cold winter. It had snowed, melted, and then frozen again, so instead of a white Christmas, we had an "ice" Christmas. That Christmas Day, my family, as was our tradition, went home to celebrate. My parents' house was built on a hill facing north, so the driveway and the adjacent parking area remained iced-over several days after most of the snow had melted. To get to the house safely, we had to park on the street and walk through a neighbor's yard, taking the long way around to my mom's back door.

Two of my cousins were there to celebrate with the family as well. They were married and had small children: one preschooler and one baby. As they were leaving later that Christmas Day, my mother and I peeked out the front window to watch them wind their way around safely to the street and their cars.

As they were carefully making their way across the icy yard and drive, I took notice of the two daddies carrying their small children. They were definitely in a precarious position, carrying their precious cargo and making sure they did not fall, but somehow I felt no apprehension or fear for them as they went. Somehow I knew there was no way they were going to allow themselves to fall and risk injury to those sweet little babies.

This is a perfect picture of how God carries us. When we allow Him to carry us through the storms and dangers of life, there is no way He is going to fall and risk injuring His precious cargo. Those babies were completely relaxed and allowed their daddies to carry them—no struggle, no fighting—and in their daddies' capable and loving arms, they made it safely to their cars.

At this realization, I declared right then and there that I wanted God to take me wherever He wanted me to go. I decided to let Him carry me, that I wouldn't struggle against what He wanted for me and would be confident of my safe arrival to His appointed destination, no matter how precarious the journey. As I stood at the window with my mother on that frozen Christmas morning, vowing this in silent prayer, little did I know that I was headed for the test and journey of my lifetime. In three short months, my mom would very suddenly pass away. Our family Christmases and life together would be changed forever, but Father would take me through it.

Tucked safely away in the will of God is the safest place in the universe. No matter what the dangers, no matter what the trial, no matter what the devastation we experience as we traverse this life, riding on Father's shoulders is the only way to arrive home safely. My Christmas wish for you is that you are there with me, tucked away in that safe place as you allow Father to carry you upon His shoulders, and headed safely home.

Prayer: *You are always there, Father, in the darkness and in the light. You are there when it is cold, when it is lonely, and when it is hard. You have been with me in the deep abyss, and You have brought me back again into the light. There are no words to describe the beauty and safety of Your presence and Your loving care. Amen.*

His Children's New Clothes

I will greatly rejoice in the LORD, my soul shall be joyful in my God; for He has clothed me with the garments of salvation, He has covered me with the robe of righteousness, as a bridegroom decks himself with ornaments, and as a bride adorns herself with her jewels.
Isaiah 61:10

After the death of my mother, we felt it was important to change a few Christmas traditions. Some of the old ones made us miss her more, so we began a new tradition of going to a movie on the afternoon of Christmas Day. Going to a movie was something we rarely did as a family, so it became a new fun adventure for us and a distraction from the loss. It helped chase away those after-Christmas blues that come when all the presents are open and the excitement has faded.

One Christmas while we were standing in the concessions line at the theater, I took notice that everything my daughter, Sally, was wearing was brand-new, from her jewelry to her shoes. She had put on all her new finery she had found under the tree that morning and had opened with much vigor and enthusiasm. She was showing off her new clothes.

I looked around and noticed the others in the lines around us. I could actually tell which people had on new clothes and which ones didn't. It wasn't because of the condition of the clothes themselves; it was their persona—their demeanor, the expressions on their faces, and their posture. I know that feeling. I've worn a brand-new outfit too, and it made me feel like I was brand-new—younger, more vibrant, fresh. I could see the manifestation of this on the faces and in the manner of these people surrounding me on Christmas Day.

When we receive the gift of salvation, we are made new. We identify with Jesus—His death, burial, and resurrection. We take it on for ourselves. The Scriptures say we have been crucified with Him. He is now clothed in the garments of a king and sits at the right hand of Father, God Almighty. Spiritually speaking, we are also seated there with Him and are clothed as He is.

We receive His righteousness; our old, dead self-righteousness has passed away. We take on a new persona, that of royalty and the humble forgiven. We can hold our heads high and look at the world and life with fresh, bold eyes. We learn to live with a clean heart and become the hands, the feet, the voice of Jesus to a world that is spiritually living in filthy rags.

Just like wearing the same outfit we received a few Christmases ago, it is easy to forget the new clothing, the fresh feeling. That persona can revert. We can get old, stale, and raggedy in our spirits. We don't forget the beauty of that brand-new outfit and how it made us feel, but it's easy to get tired of wearing it and put it in the back of the closet where we don't see it or try it on very often.

We are not useful to God in the back of the closet. We need to be reminded that with Him every day is brand-new. We are still His new creations, and as long as we seek His forgiveness daily and stay in fellowship with Him, we show the world *His* persona. When we do, we'll probably stand a little straighter, and it's just like having a new outfit to wear every single day.

Prayer: *I ask You to forgive me, Lord, for the times I've allowed my walk with You to become stale and old hat. I thank You for that wonderful feeling of newness that You are able to bring to me every day. Amen.*

A Love Such as This

For Jean, Joanne, Janet, and Polly

For God so loved the world that He gave His only begotten Son, that whoever believes in Him should not perish but have everlasting life.
John 3:16

I don't think we can get a really clear picture of what *sacrifice* is until we have children of our own. It wasn't until I was a mother myself that I began to comprehend the sacrificial love my parents had for me as a child.

It was Sunday morning, December 10, 1967. I was only ten years old. Daddy was stationed at Randolph Air Force Base in San Antonio, Texas. I had been sick and was sitting at the kitchen table catching up on math homework. Fractions—I hated them then and still do now. The phone rang, and it was my mother's uncle calling from Nashville. My mom answered the phone, and he immediately asked to speak to my dad. This sent my mom into an emotional tailspin—she knew this meant there had to be terrible news to share.

On the way to church that morning, my grandparents were involved in a head-on collision with a woman who was also driving to church with her three grandchildren aboard. My grandmother, the other driver, and two of her grandchildren (a two-year-old and a five-year-old) were killed instantly. The third child and my grandfather were the only survivors, and both were in a critical state.

We quickly closed up the house and drove a grueling seventeen hours home to Nashville. My mom arrived at the hospital just before my grandfather was taken into surgery on Monday morning. She was able to kiss him, tell him she loved him, and grieve momentarily with him over the loss of my grandmother. He did not survive the surgery. Mercifully, the third child survived this horrendous accident and eventually healed completely.

My grandparents were in the prime of life and very healthy, but they were taken from us all in this one tragic instant. No one could have had any expectation of something like this happening. My grandparents had not planned ahead, and so began a long month of taking care of estate issues and other necessary formalities. It was a dramatic time, one that dwells in my memory as vividly as if it were yesterday. The depth of sadness and deep longing to be able to turn back time and have my grandparents back with us was profound; it was that initial time of grieving where denial and bargaining consumed our days. We were all staying together in a household of darkness and loss. I was so young, but I knew that the vacant look in my mother's eyes was something I would never forget.

It took the entire month of December and into early January to get things finalized, but my three cousins and I were not forgotten during that time of such utter sadness and deep mourning. Less than two weeks after the funeral, a Christmas tree went up in my grandparents' living room, and on Christmas morning, we awoke to find that Santa Claus had indeed visited all four of the children in that traumatized home.

As small children, it was natural for us to assume that of course Santa Claus would come on Christmas Eve. Until I was grown with children of my own, I did not understand the sacrifice it was for my mom and her sisters to produce a Christmas celebration for us while so grief-stricken from the loss of their parents. A celebration was the farthest thing from their minds and hearts, but they did it for us. This time of selfless devotion was my initial lesson in sacrificial love.

As an adult, putting the needs and wishes of my children ahead of my own came naturally to me. That is what this love is all about; it presents a clear picture of how God looks upon us as His children. He sacrificed His only Son for the sake of His creation, mankind. He put Himself aside for us and became a man who lived, died, and rose again so that we could have eternal life with Him in heaven. Putting us first is why Jesus came, and His decision to do so is the true meaning of Christmas.

I try to remember this each and every Christmas season when I get too busy and stressed. I remember the sacrifice my parents, aunts, and uncles made for me, and I keep a promise I made to my mother by telling this story every year to anyone who will listen—to honor her and my grandparents, and to pass on the true joy that comes from a love such as this and from sacrificing yourself for others.

Prayer: *Life is full of losses, Father. No one knows that better than You. Bless You, Lord, for walking with us through the losses of life and for sacrificing so much for us. Amen.*

Y2K = Yes to the King

These things I have written to you who believe in the name of the Son of God, that you may know that you have eternal life.
1 John 5:13

Do you remember Y2K? It was all we talked about the last two years of the twentieth century, but now it is only a distant memory. I wrote this one week before the turn of the century and I saved this entry for last because facing the future with certainty is always relevant, and that makes it the perfect epilogue as you close this book and move on. I hope something written here has resonated with you and will continue to do so. Be blessed.

I am writing this on Christmas Day 1999 for several reasons. One, the guys are hogging the TV and I have some time on my hands, but the main reason is that I don't want to "cheat" and write this *after* I know the outcome when the clock turns to midnight one week from now. No matter how many experts or naysayers I listen to, it is still a fact that no one truly knows what is going to happen, if anything, and to what degree. Y2K could end up being a big nothing, or it might be a big something. Who's to say?

God, that's who! He knows exactly what is going to happen and when it will happen. No matter the century, millennium, or eon, He knows it all. I am writing this from the vantage point of knowing nothing about the coming new year, but then, isn't that the way it is every year? Do we ever know what the new year will bring, what will happen to us or to the ones we know and love? It's always a big mystery. Here we have been anticipating and preparing for the year 2000 with a larger than usual interest and expectation (and in some cases, panic), but it really is no different from any other new year when looked at from God's perspective. He knows, we don't, and that's that!

At this same time last year, I had no idea that I had just spent my last Christmas with my mom. God knew it, but I didn't. To me, losing her was so much greater than Y2K could ever be. But, you know, no matter what tragedy or disaster lies around the corner, God doesn't want us to live our lives as though we are about to experience something catastrophic. How do I know this? He says so in the Bible. God says He wants us to be assured of the certainties that are God-given, and I believe that is the way He wants us to live—walking, and resting, in those assurances.

I have two promises in particular I want to share with you. One is Jeremiah 33:20–21, which essentially says that as surely as day and night will go on and on until the end of the world, so will God keep His promises. He doesn't go back on His word, and time will march on. The second is found in 1 John 5:13, which tells us that God wants us to be assured of our eternal life.

Will you be spending the next year (or years) worried about the uncertainties of life (and perhaps your eternal life), or will you rest, certain in the things He has promised? I've lived both ways, and I have to tell you, the latter is by far the sweeter and more victorious way to live.

Read on, and you will find information and a prayer for you if you are uncertain about your future. If you pray this prayer with a sincere heart, God will forgive you of all your sins. You'll become His child and will receive the gift of eternal life, plus the bonus of a life on earth that is filled with a certainty you can count on.

Prayer: *Father, please bless every person who has taken time to read this book. Bless them in their coming and their going. Bless their families, their homes, and their lives. May they be with You, and may they know the incredible peace and presence of the Almighty in the precious name of Jesus Christ. Amen.*

Do You Know?

1. Eternal life is a free gift from God.
   God loves you and wants to give you this gift.
   You cannot earn or deserve it.
2. Man cannot save himself, because he is a sinner.
   Sin means you have fallen short of God's perfection.
3. God is merciful and doesn't want to punish us, but He is also just
   and therefore must punish sin.
   We've all sinned; the penalty for sin is death, and the penalty
   must be paid.
4. God became a man, Jesus.
   He lived a sinless life on earth for us, then took the punishment
   for our sin on the cross.
5. We receive the gift of eternal life by faith.
   This faith is trusting in Jesus Christ alone for our salvation.
   We rest on what He has done, rather than on what we've done
   to get us into heaven.

If you want to receive this gift, pray this prayer:

Dear Lord Jesus,

*I believe You are the Son of God and that You suffered upon the cross,
died, and rose again. I know I have sinned, and I ask you to forgive me. I
now turn from my sins and receive You as my Lord and Savior. Thank You,
Lord, for the gift of eternal life. Amen.*

The Purpose of the Parables

*A*nd the disciples came and said to Him, "Why do You speak to them in parables?"

He answered and said to them, "Because it has been given to you to know the mysteries of the kingdom of heaven, but to them it has not been given. For whoever has, to him more will be given, and he will have abundance; but whoever does not have, even what he has will be taken away from him. Therefore I speak to them in parables, because seeing they do not see, and hearing they do not hear, nor do they understand. And in them the prophecy of Isaiah is fulfilled, which says:

> *'Hearing you will hear and shall not understand,*
> *And seeing you will see and not perceive;*
> *For the hearts of this people have grown dull.*
> *Their ears are hard of hearing,*
> *And their eyes they have closed,*
> *Lest they should see with their eyes and hear with their ears,*
> *Lest they should understand with their hearts and turn,*
> *So that I should heal them.'*

"But blessed are your eyes for they see, and your ears for they hear; for assuredly, I say to you that many prophets and righteous men desired to see what you see, and did not see it, and to hear what you hear, and did not hear it."

Matthew 13:10–17

About the Author

Judy Grenley holds a PhD in clinical Christian counseling. She lives in Old Hickory, Tennessee, with her husband of thirty-six years, Michael, and their two dogs, Arlo and Sunny. They have two grown children, Sally and Will, and an equally grown son-in-law, Daniel, all of whom they adore. They attend church at World Outreach Church in Murfreesboro, Tennessee, and find that each new day has another parable just waiting to be shared.

CPSIA information can be obtained at www.ICGtesting.com
Printed in the USA
LVOW08s0310090316

478337LV00001B/1/P

9 781498 465649